Journeys

To: Kurt and Sanda —
With all good wishes.

Ernest.

3-4-14

Journeys

Survival is the Best Revenge

Ernest Feibelman

To order additional copies of this book, contact:
Xlibris Corporation
1-888-795-4274
www.Xlibris.com
Orders@Xlibris.com
74837

CONTENTS

Statement by the Author i

Acknowledgments iii

Introduction..v

Preface..ix

Chapter 1—Escape to Belgium 1

Chapter 2—Brussels..4

Chapter 3—Back to Brussels 8

Chapter 4—France...13

Chapter 5—La Republique Francaise 16

Chapter 6—Narrow Escape..24

Chapter 7—Switzerland 29

Chapter 8—Katie's Choice 33

Chapter 9—St. Gallen and the Neuburger Family..............36

Chapter 10—The Correspondence 41

Chapter 11—Camp Montana 51

Chapter 12—The Family 57

Chapter 13—"Papa" 72

Chapter 14—Victory. But, The Journey Continues.............77

Chapter 15—America—Part I..91

Chapter 16—America—Part II 105

Chapter 17—A Final Return to Mannheim 123

Epilogue...127

STATEMENT BY THE AUTHOR

Dear Family and Friends:

Due to my dear mother's blessed advanced age, time is of the essence. I am, therefore, self-publishing this book as expeditiously as possible for the limited readership implied above. We (mother and I) are fortunate to have many documents, letters, family trees, and photographs which, unfortunately, and again in the interest of time, I cannot be reproduced as a part of this printing. However, in the narrative, these "papers" will be parenthetically marked "Exhibit", and can—in a limited way—be sent to you upon request. Should there be any interest for a second, i.e. commercial and expanded printing, these "exhibits" would naturally be included.

Thank you for your understanding.

I am consigning this book to you with my best wishes.

*   *   *

I've become increasingly concerned about the way the Holocaust has been misused and abused in public discourse. This is a serious issue because it minimizes the evil of Nazism, insults the memory of the victims of the Holocaust, and has the potential to further inflame present-day anti-Semitism. Yet, this is not the time for cynicism and inaction. Please spread this urgent message, and—with me—aggressively pursue honoring the memory of the victims, to counter Holocaust denial and anti-Semitism, and speak out against the trivialization of the unparalleled human tragedy that we call The Holocaust.

My thanks go out for your steadfast support now and in the future, with special gratitude to my many kind and loyal friends of all religious persuasions.

ACKNOWLEDGMENTS

My sincerest thanks go out to those who assisted me in the writing of *Journeys*:

To my dear mother, who retold her dramatic story to me in a series of interviews and re-inspired me to take on this venture.

To my late uncle, Alfred Strauss, who guided me with his accurate, excellent advice, while filling in some missing facts, places and dates.

To my cousins, Debbie Strauss and Bill Bame, who diligently and competently edited this manuscript for spelling, syntax and grammar.

To my good friend, William "Bill" Crerend, for his guidance, contributions and for his remarkably sensitive, emotional, yet erudite overview of the Holocaust.

To yet another dear friend, Retired Major General (U.S. Army) Jerry R. Curry, who graciously assisted in the early, formative stage of this book.

And finally to my dear wife, Harriet, friend and companion through life, for her patience and understanding during the slow—and at times difficult—birth of this project.

*   *   *

I acknowledge that in addition to my dearly beloved mother, I dedicate this book to my darling grandchildren: to Abbi, in this, the year of her Bat Mitzvah, and to Julia, and to their generation. They will soon be the leaders of our people, our country and the world. May they never forget!

INTRODUCTION

"The [Third Reich] was inaugurated in peacetime, and
peacefully, by the Germans themselves, out of both their
weaknesses and their strengths. The Germans imposed the Nazi
tyranny on themselves. Many of them, perhaps a majority,
did not realize it was at that noon hour of January 30, 1933,
when President Hindenburg, acting in perfectly constitutional
manner, entrusted the chancellorship to Adolph Hitler.
But, they were soon to learn." William Shirer—1960

My mother and I are Holocaust survivors. My dear mother, still going strong at the age of one hundred and one, saved my life by saving her own. It is for this reason that this book is lovingly and admiringly dedicated to her. I had long intended to put her memoirs on paper. About four years ago I interviewed my mother on several successive Sunday afternoons. I marveled at the documents, letters and pictures that had survived in her care.

I am finally at the last stage of completing this book, the story of her brave and courageous life, entitled *Journeys*.

However, a book can itself be a journey, in that it doesn't always take the intended course. Although it seems like the ultimate hubris to suddenly start writing about oneself, I felt that our story cannot be told in a one-dimensional manner. Beginning at the age of eight, my life was no longer exclusively intertwined with my mother's. A new cast of actors entered upon the stage of our lives, namely the Neuburgers, my Swiss foster parents and their sons. My urge to re-examine my own life in this tripartite prism grew more pressing. My concern became to provide a clear picture of what befell us—and the other important members of the wider family—amid the horrors of the Holocaust. Further, *Journeys* is intended to serve as both an anatomy and an indictment of the strident, indecent, arrogant, fanatic, lunatic, bizarre and murderous German nation from 1933 to 1945.

However, let there be no doubt about it! This is primarily my mother's story: Kate Hecht born in Mannheim, Germany on September 13, 1908, maiden name Strauss, married to Leon Feibelmann, a distant cousin, in 1933, and remarried to Edmond Hecht in 1953. And, yes, this is yet another Holocaust story. It is the author's full intention to write a personal story of my mother's—and her family's—experiences during the worst of times. It is intended to be an intimate narrative, not a polemic, nor a detailed, scholarly examination of the history of the Holocaust, or the complete history of Nazi-Germany and modern Europe. It's just storytelling, albeit about a very tragic tale about our family and our fellow-European Jews. There are millions of Holocaust stories. Each one is different. Each one needs to be told. Each one needs to be remembered. This is—and must be—my mother's story because she was at the center of the storm. She was the decision-maker, the mover-and-shaker in the family, especially after November 1938. It is in that sense that my mother played the central role in the fortunes of the family from this point forward, frequently among the saddest misfortune. Always, the ardent pro-emigrationist, she would grow from strength to greater strength. A woman of wisdom and energy, she would operate on the theory of "attitude—dedication—results". She would manage the impossible with vision, resourcefulness, resilience, determination and an always-optimistic outlook on life. She inhabits this tale. She is the heroine of these collected memories. And, how fortunate we are to call her that.

As for this book, we—mother and I—aim to shun the pyrotechnics and the sensational, yet impart the aura of lethal danger that enveloped us every day. As for the prose, we are not interested in the artful, the lyrical or the euphonious. We are interested only in valid and sincere reporting. And foremost, do not expect to find resolution. My mother had to be prepared to cross rocky, rough terrain, which she would accomplish with unflinching resolve and competence. Hitler, his Nazi Party, his "inner circle", the aristocracy, the military and the overwhelming majority of the German people were about to transgress against human life itself. Their actions had the most tragic impact on our lives. But, my mother persevered, survived, and in time prospered.

Coping with daily life in the early years of the Nazi regime and finding the correct focus on the future was a matter of mindset because the deterioration of conditions for the Jews was incremental. Germany hosted the 1936 Olympics. The true nature of the horror to come was still well-disguised. During the early years of the Nazi regime, the majority of German Jews were anti-emigration and neutral on Zionism. Only one in ten German Jews was active in the Zionist movement with a possible interest to settle in Palestine. And America? America seemed far away. America was a place to send the black sheep of the family. America represented a foreign culture and a foreign language.

However, by 1938 it was too late to be pro-active. Jews now became re-active. They had now been disenfranchised for more than three years. The grave and imminent danger set in. On *Kistallnacht*, November 9, 1938, the nationwide pogrom night in Germany, my father was arrested in our home. He was shipped to Dachau, the concentration camp located in a suburb of Munich. Even pre-war Dachau was not just a "detention center" or "jail". Jews in Dachau were routinely beaten, tortured and murdered. When my father returned from Dachau in early 1939, he was but a shadow of his former self. He had been beaten and tortured. He regularly awakened from terrible nightmares. He was disoriented and depressed. How could this happen to a decorated Word War One veteran of the German Army? He was in no condition to lead the family. Now, more than ever, that role had to be carried out by my mother. At this late stage in the game, there could be no more compromise or procrastination.

However, the story goes back further. My parents were married on December 28, 1933. Their marriage certificate (*Heiratsurkunde*) is evidence that the winds of change. Fascism and official state-sponsored anti-Semitism were blowing fast and hard just months after Hitler's installation as Chancellor. The certificate already "assigns" the names of Israel and Sara to the couple, and bears the Swastika seal. (See Exhibit—hereafter indicated merely as "Exh.")

Emigration should have been Priority One for a young, affluent couple. But there were many distractions and diversions. My father married into my mother's family business. An excellent salesman and business man himself, he now dedicated himself to being fully integrated into his new business environment. In 1934, my grandfather died prematurely. My father now had to run the business. Later that year, my mother's much younger brother, Alfred, had his Bar Mitzvah. Although this was the last time the entire extended family was together, it was not an entirely joyous event. The younger generation had more day-to-day contact with the Nazis: beatings by classmates; overt expressions of anti-Semitism by teachers who had already joined the Nazi party and taught proudly dressed in their S.A. uniforms. As a result of these deteriorating conditions, tensions in the family surfaced on the matter of emigration. There were in fact pro-emigration and anti-emigration protagonists within the closest circle of the family. But, more—much more—will be said about this posturing in the pages to follow.

On December 30, 1934, a son was born.

*   *   *

Although I dared to interject my personality into "the story", I eschewed a professional editor. These remembrances will not be reviewed by book critics. This volume is directed at my family, nuclear and extended, my good friends and anyone who will listen . . . and, hopefully, will not forget.

*   *   *

About the author.

1934

In 1934 Cavalcade won the Kentucky Derby, and St. Louis won the World Series. "It Happened One Night" swept the Academy Awards. Hank Aaron, Ralph Nader, Gloria Steinem, Sophia Loren, Brigitte Bardot, and Carl Sagan were born.

However, 1934 was not a good year for a Jewish child to be born in Germany. The birth certificate carries the Seal of the Swastika. The middle name, Israel, was automatically and systematically "assigned" to every Jewish newborn male. My birth certificate reads Ernst Israel Feibelmann. (Exh.)

The beginning of the end for European Jewry had already begun.

PREFACE

The German *"Volk"*—1870 to 1933:
From Skepticism to Nihilism

My mother describes her pre-Nazi years to have passed like those of any other Jewish girl from the relatively comfortable merchant class. The "Golden Age" of German Jewry, best described as urbanization and assimilation, began after the Franco-Prussian War victory and Bismarck's ascension. World War One interrupted these idyllic years with nightly Allied bombardments in the industrial twin-city of Mannheim-Ludwigshafen. Six years of age, and scared, mother was always first to reach the cellar. The family survived unscathed. Immediately after WWI, there were food and fuel shortages. But, in a family business that dealt in a commodity, there were always opportunities to barter. In the last year or two of the war, my mother happily went to summer camp, out of harm's way, with plenty of fresh air and constant games and physical activities. And, when you were tired and hungry, you ate pretty much whatever was served. She went to public school and later attended a private all-girls' school. She had blond pigtails and was often mistaken for her Christian counterparts, with whom she played at school and at home. In other words, her young days were conventional. She loved swimming, bicycling, and other sports and very much fit in. Mother claims that as a child she did not experience overt anti-Semitism. Further, she told me, that teachers' likes and dislikes of pupils, were not based on religious bias, but rather on individual preference. Nevertheless, mother adds—and accepts—that there was always an undertone of "benign" anti-Semitism in Germany and throughout Europe. A wonderful photograph of my mother at age sixteen or seventeen survives. ("Exh".). In her late teen and young-adult years she blossomed within a tightly knit group of Jewish boys and girls, friends and cousins. They swam and danced; they partied and laughed . . . and worked. It was the German version of The Roaring Twenties. In this crowd, one didn't worry too much about the Versailles Treaty and its menacing after-effects; or about hyper-inflation (Again, the barter network and a continuous flow of earnings from the business—in the currency of the day, good or bad—helped a great deal.); or about Hitler's 1923 Beer Hall Putch; or the early appearance of Hitler's newspaper, the *Voeklischer Beobachter*. However, once the Nazi threat became overt, no one's antennae were more accurately receptive than my mother's.

The German people may have been skeptical at first. But soon they slowly but surely fell under the baffling and disarming spell of the Nazi Party. The Nazis became increasingly suspect to becoming the culprit in Germany's murderous future. Yet, even those who at first may have resisted—or, indeed, recoiled from the rule of the new regime—soon fell prey to incipient Nazi propaganda, intimidation, and the fallout of virulent social repression. That after all is what they chose.

This became the new environment of the German Jew. Soon, difficult decisions would have to be made. Life is not crystalline. It is full of secrets.

CHAPTER 1

Escape to Belgium

"The world seems to be divided into two: Places where Jews can't live, and places which Jews can't enter." Chaim Weizman—1936

The 1936 Berlin Olympiads that began on August 1, 1936 were in the history books. Time moved on swiftly and treacherously. The "Winds of War", to use Churchill's famous book title, were blowing. The clouds of war and persecution and evil were gathering and moving irreversibly. The sky was dark, awaiting the historic calamity to come. Affidavits and exit permits were—now more than ever—the center of attention for Germany's Jews. Meanwhile, and even prior to the Olympics, the host nation had already opened four Nazi concentration camps in Germany. Boycotts of Jewish shops and businesses had been staged. The Nazi's Aryan (and non-Aryan) decrees were issued. Burning books in Berlin and throughout Germany became a Nazi hobby. The Nazis prohibited Jews from owning land. Jews are prohibited from being newspaper editors. Jews were no longer permitted to participate in national health insurance. Jews were prohibited from getting legal qualifications. In August of 1934, upon Hindenburg's death, Hitler becomes "*Fuehrer*", with ninety percent of Germans voting 'yes' and thereby approving his new powers. Next, the Nazis banned Jews from serving in the military. The infamous Nuremberg Laws against the Jews were decreed. In February 1936, the German Gestapo was placed above the law.

Shortly after the Olympic Games, the Jews were banned from most professional occupations, including teaching Germans and the accounting and dentistry professions. Hitler's *Anschluss* (union) with Austria, and Nazi troops entering Austria on March 12, 1938, doomed the Austrian Jewish population of 200,000, mainly living in Vienna. In Germany, Jewish-owned businesses, wealth and property were ordered to be "registered". In July 1938, a League of Nations conference, with delegates from thirty-two nations, assembled at Evian, France to consider helping Jews fleeing Hitler. It ended in inaction as no country would take them. At this time, Jewish physicians in Germany were prohibited by law to practice medicine. German law required Jewish passports to be stamped with a large red "J". (The Germans had some help from the Swiss on that, thank you very much.) Just over five months before the start of World War Two, Nazi troops seized Czechoslovakia with its Jewish population of 350,00 Jews. By now, the Jews of Germany had just about lost all their rights and privileges. The *St. Louis,* the infamous ship crowded with 930 Jewish refugees, was turned away by Cuba and the United States and forced to return to Europe. In Great Britain and France the outbreak of war is deemed to be imminent and unavoidable. It is high time for every Jew remaining in Germany to flee, be it legally or illegally!

On September 1, 1939, Germany attacked and invaded Poland by land and by air, marking the beginning of World War Two in The West. Just two-and-a-half weeks prior to that date the Feibelmann family, Leon, his wife Kate, and son Ernst (not quite five years old) attempted an illegal border crossing from Germany to Belgium. They boarded a train in Mannheim, their home town, and traveled to Cologne. Changing trains, they continued to Aachen, a city near the Belgian border. A street car went to the border. Without luggage, the Feibelmanns boarded the street car, intending to get off at the second to last stop. There, by precise pre-arrangement, Belgian friends by the name of Schloss, were to meet us and transport us by car across the Belgian border and on to Brussels. They were Belgian nationals, having left Germany much earlier, and by this time owned and operated the Café Schloss in Brussels. As an extra precaution, Ellie Schloss accompanied us on the street car, while her husband, Arthur, waited in his car on the Belgian side of the border. We got off at the wrong stop and of course missed our "guide" Arthur.

With war approaching, the Gestapo and the SS had just begun to man many border crossings. Although new in their assignment, they nevertheless knew that this border crossing had the potential of a "popular" escape route. Ellie, the Belgian citizen, pretended not to be part of our little family group. However, Kate, Leon and Ernst were arrested. My father was sent to the local prison. Mother and I were taken by car to a Catholic convent in Aachen. The nuns were sympathetic, and hoping no harm would come to us kindly provided a bedroom and breakfast. Fear and shock engulfed my mother.

Upon awakening from a brief and restless sleep, she was surprised—in her own words—that her hair had not turned white overnight. After breakfast, two members of the S.A., the *Sturmabteilung* (storm troopers), which many consider the midwife of the Nazi takeover of the German nation, in uniform, complete with the infamous arm band of red ground with the black swastika, arrived to deliver us—again by car—to the Police Chief of Aachen. They left us in his care. Interrogation followed. My mother promised to return to Mannheim, seemingly a satisfactory reply. The police chief contacted the local jail and ordered that my father be released. He further promised my mother that her husband would meet her at the Aachen train station. He kept his word. My mother tells me that I asked why we had to flee. Her answer: "They want us dead because we were born into the wrong religion."

However, we only went back to Cologne and headed for the home of Arthur Schloss' mother. My father had known this elderly lady for over twenty years. In a period of history, when time itself became a matter of life and death, two fretful weeks were to pass. During this time our good friends Arthur and Ellie Schloss arranged for Belgian passports for us on the "black market". So, back to Aachen. However, this time we crossed the border on a late-night train headed for Brussels. German passport control, followed by their Belgian counterparts, passed through the train. We showed our ersatz Belgian passports, and they passed muster! The Schloss' picked us up at the train station, and we stayed at their apartment until able to find our own. It was August 28, 1939, three days before the massive German Guns of September fired their first shells in earnest and World War Two began. Eleventh-hour negotiations between Great Britain and Germany failed. The time-specific British ultimatum expired. Almost by default, the world—especially European Jewry—slipped into disaster and would never be the same.

CHAPTER 2

Brussels

. . . and "the Deliverance of Dunkirk", to quote Winston Churchill.

Since Germany was about to begin hostilities on the Eastern front, the Benelux countries would not be invaded until the following year. We found Brussels to be a beautiful and classically European city. We stayed with the Schloss family for a few days, while my parents looked for an apartment and handled the paperwork chores. As for the latter, my parents registered with the Brussels police, who—after the usual background check—issued a residency permit dated October 20, 1939. (Exh.) My parents found and rented a furnished efficiency apartment, with kitchen: 82 Rue Vanderschrick. It was clean and tidy, in a neat building in a pleasant neighborhood. The landlady, a Madame Preiser, was a lovely person. Her husband had been dispatched to the Belgian Congo and—as we learned later—did not return to Brussels until 1943. My mother took up correspondence with Mrs. Preiser shortly before we immigrated to America in 1946. A single letter survived in my mother's files.

To pay for all this, my parents transferred funds from a small remaining balance of a Swiss bank account to a Belgian bank. The Swiss bank account was with the banking firm of Julius Baer & Co., Zurich. The account bore five percent interest. The money helped to establish some semblance of normalcy while we marked time. My parents enrolled me in a nearby public school, Ecole St. Gilles. The game plan was simple: Sit and wait for our United States quota number to come up, and exit Belgium by ship as quickly as possible by way of a Belgian port city. Unfortunately, United States immigration policy was restrictive and slow by design. The quota was minute. Considering that the war had already started, and being aware of the enormous, lethal dangers facing European Jewry, this policy was—in a word—unconscionable. Except for a few old-money, Republican Jewish-American families, the vast majority of American Jews loved Roosevelt while in office and deified him after his death. From the point of view of European Jewry, he failed.

So, we waited and waited and waited. Surprisingly, the German Consulate in Brussels issued a new passport to my mother—also covering me—on October 17, 1939, and again on February 16, 1940 for one year. (Exh.) The details of those incidents will be covered in the pages to follow. At least for now, the waiting ended abruptly on May 10, 1940, when Germany, bypassing the Maginot Line, and without warning, invaded Belgium and the other Benelux countries. The entire Belgian population became refugees attempting to outrun the German Blitzkrieg. The refugees' goal was to cross the border into France. Though probably well-intended, sadly the Belgian government made arrangements for all adult Jewish males to be transported, by train, to Southern France for "their own safety". The French quickly set up internment camps for this first wave of refugees. My father was among these refugees. Belgium's policy was not voluntary. My mother and I—and other Jewish families—joined the Belgian exodus, attempting to blend in as well as possible. Generally, the fleeing Belgian population intended to head west and cross the French border. Those who did not have cars or trucks or bicycles or farm carts, such as my mother and me and thousands more, traveled by train. You can imagine the huge crowds and turmoil at the train station. My mother intended to head for Southern France in an attempt to reunite with my father. However, chaos and confusion ruled, and we ended up on a train heading for Calais via Abbeville, both on the French coast. The German Luftwaffe routinely stopped these trains by inflicting rail damage, strafed the trains with automatic weapons and simultaneously bombed them. German spies, dressed as priests and riding with the refugees signaled the German flyers, alerting them to French troops and/or war materiel aboard the train. If and when this was the case, the Luftwaffe intensified its attack with total disregard for the civilians packing these trains to—and beyond—the limit. We were on one such train. I remember the incident clearly . . . and always will. When the passengers became aware of the intensity of the attack, they detrained in great haste and attempted to seek some cover and shelter in the ditches running parallel to the tracks. The pilots now redirected their fire to include these ditches. Who would die and who would survive simply became a game of Russian roulette: the only constant in conventional warfare. However, later, the herding of helpless, innocent, naked Jewish men, women and children into lethal gas chambers and/or ovens was hardly conventional warfare; neither was starvation and non-benign neglect. The odds for survival change. More about that in the pages to follow . . . much more. The French railroad workers, with the help of some refugees, managed to get the train restarted and continue its run towards Calais and the English Channel.

A few days later, on May 17, 1940, Germany invaded France. Although reinforced by a sizeable British Expeditionary Force, the French Army was no match for the massive, rapid German attack. The German Wehrmacht was like a tsunami, and—unbeknownst to us—outflanked the mass of refugees, now swollen by fleeing Frenchmen, running in the same direction, namely westward. The German army was already nearing the English Channel, attacking from two sides. The entire coastal area of Northwestern France became a battleground. The Allies were caught in a deadly pincer movement. Shock and awe and "overwhelming strength" hit the Allies like so many knockout punches. (No, my esteemed alumnus, Colin Powell, did not invent that doctrine of warfare.) The Germans made Dunkirk their central focal point. Due to the fierce fighting, our train was unable to enter Calais. The mass of humanity detrained. In doing so, it separated into small groups. We joined a group of about a hundred "Belgian" refugees, Gentile and Jewish. In the chaos that is war, we did not know in which direction to flee. Nonetheless, we were actually heading towards Calais, a town near Dunkirk. Once within the city limits, we made contact with the local police, who were trying to guide the refugees to "places of safety", as the battle approached closer and closer. A policeman escorted our group to a school gym. It was May 25, 1940. The retreating British troops offered us some food, which was gladly received. Once again, we waited helplessly, while we heard the sounds of battle intensifying. Backed to the wall, in the form of the English Channel that is, the British fighting men were stiffening their resistance. We huddled in that gym for three days.

Suddenly, the door swung open and a Captain of the German Wehrmacht, obviously not a Nazi fanatic, burst into the gym, in total surprise and disbelief at what he saw: people, civilians. One of the Gentile Belgians approached him and explained our plight. The Captain realized that there were Jews embedded among the Belgians. He almost diplomatically implied that he had no intention of harming them. He had bigger game to pursue. He quickly said that we could not possibly stay at the schoolhouse. In an hour's time it would not be standing, he said. He summoned his sergeant, and instructed him to make every attempt to guide us safely through the battle zone, out of the city, and behind German lines. Miraculously, he (and we) succeeded. We did not realize that back at the coast the name Dunkirk would enter the history books forever.

In an act of further kindness, the sergeant stayed with us. We walked to a village about six miles past the city line. At this point our group numbered only about thirty people, again consisting of Belgian Jews and Gentiles. Some of the refugees preferred to distance themselves from the German sergeant. He led us into the farm country east of Calais. In this surreal universe, the German sergeant knocked on the local farmers' doors to request shelter for the alien people he was charged to protect . . . a few here, a few there, further splitting up the group into family units, men, women and children that may have been "on the run" together all along, and refugees who became friends on the journey. Friendships bond quickly when exposed to constant danger while sharing a common enemy. My mother had a special talent in making friends and forming potentially important associations. We stayed in the stables. The French farmers supplied blankets. Surprisingly, most people had some money. We paid the farmers for the food they were able to supply. Everything else we purchased in the village. We stayed about two-and-a-half weeks, while the railroad's rails and rail beds damaged by the bombing were being repaired. The German Army, concentrating on their priorities, did not interfere with our movements. And so, it was back to Brussels for my mother and me. We had nowhere else to go.

CHAPTER 3

Back to Brussels

The Young Lion.

My mother and I returned to a changed city. Conquered, occupied cities tend to turn gray overnight. Fear and uncertainty hung in the air like a precursor to the smog that plagues the cities of today. German troops and huge German flags and banners were intentionally visible everywhere. My mother and I returned to our apartment. We were once again in limbo only now without a husband and father. On December 16, 1940, mother had the unthinkable fortitude and outright chutzpah to once again go to the German Consulate and request renewal of her passport, replete with the big red "J" and the unwanted additional middle name, Sara. Again, the vagaries of war: They renewed the passport with typical German administrative efficiency. Time moved slowly. Alone, and feeling stranded, my mother had difficulty in dealing with the sad, lingering fact that our entry-visa into the United States had not yet been granted by the American authorities. The menace of the occupying forces was immense. Survival became a spiraling, evermore stressful day-to-day existence. In the meantime at least, mother was able to maintain contact with my father, who remained interned in Southern France.

For the Jews, the situation in Belgium worsened by the hour as the Germans consolidated their military victory and the repressive, administrative and political instruments of occupation. Deportation of Jews began, at first mainly to camps in German-occupied France. It was time to get out of Brussels . . . quickly! My mother's antennae for danger and her propensity for individual motivation and immediate action came to the forefront as never before. Through the Bier family, as mother tells it, also German refugees whom my mother had befriended, mother learned that a small village near Mons was believed to be the best area to cross into Nazi-occupied France. They also informed mother that two other German refugee women of their acquaintance, each with two small children, were also planning to attempt a crossing. After speaking to yet another allegedly knowledgeable Jewish-Belgian friend, it was decided to cross the border into France at Givry because it was "reported" that this area was sparsely and irregularly patrolled by the Germans since no sizeable garrison had been established yet. Since it was easy to get lost and disoriented at night, it was recommended that the women and their children cross the border during daytime hours. When we arrived at Givry, my mother went out beyond the village to take a look at the terrain. She now had a plan in her mind and went back to fetch the other two women and the children. She decided, and the two women agreed, to attempt to cross the border by way of a narrow dirt trail that snaked its way through open farm country. It was the height of the growing season, wheat on the right, potatoes on the left. If stopped, one of the women who spoke a few words of French would say that we were just out for a walk.

It was difficult to identify the actual border. The women looked for a marker, but did not think it wise to tarry. In any event, the women agreed that they must have crossed the border by now. The fields were wide open without any real cover. Save the growing wheat, there were only some bushes and shrubs along the other field, which sloped downward and southward.

Suddenly, breaking the silence of the warm, seemingly peaceful summer afternoon, a German patrol was coming up the hill. It consisted of what immediately seemed to be an officer, a sergeant and six other members of the regular German Army, the Wehrmacht.

True to the infantry manual, they were spread out in a large diamond formation, their weapons not drawn. The sergeant was the first to spot us as we were crouching behind a bush. He called over to us in German, "What are you doing there?" No reply. The women were in total shock and trembling with fear. What seemed like the beginning of a long journey just a moment ago, may have turned into its sudden, fatal end. By now the lieutenant saw us as well and barked out the same question. The woman who spoke a little French babbled out something. Her "French act" did not impress the lieutenant. He looked like a "by-the-book" type of a warrior. He was tall, slender, blond, and young. Perhaps the reader will remember the Arian-looking lieutenant in the movie "The Young Lions" played by a very blond Marlon Brando. Well, this German kid must have been the model. He probably would have preferred to serve with *Waffen-SS*. For now he had to be content with his current assignment. Coming closer, the lieutenant, noticing the little hand luggage and bags, wanted to see proper identification cards . . . and he wanted to see them now. We were unable to produce them. We did not think that a Belgian equivalent of a green card or a German passport of the "J" variety would help in this situation. The lieutenant immediately considered us his prisoners. At once, the entire patrol acted accordingly. In other words, they got serious . . . right here and now. If earlier they seemed to be almost strolling across the quiet, peaceful, rural countryside, their bearing now assumed a stiff military look: alert and business-like. "Take them to headquarters" the lieutenant sternly said to his sergeant, who now took over. The lieutenant walked behind us and ordered the patrol—and us—to walk at a quicker pace. Knees buckling, stomachs full of butterflies, blood pressure up, the children almost running, we attempted to keep up.

We soon approached what was sure to be headquarters. Picture the old, classic French country squire's house, or perhaps that of a rich farmer. Appropriated by the German Army, it was a substantial stucco and stone house with barns and side structures. A large courtyard was surrounded by a thick fourteen-foot wall, with an immense old and imposing solid-wood door at the entrance. Once inside this wall, the lieutenant came forward and instructed us to form a semi-circle in front of him. He calmly advised us that he had decided that we were neither Belgian nor French, but rather refugees on the run, and that we were most certainly Jews. "My routine orders", he said, "are to shoot you on the spot . . . and that is precisely what I intend to do now." Turning to the sergeant, he continued: "Line them up against the wall!" As my mother tells this hair-raising story, the sergeant and his men seemed surprised, startled, tentative. The women, crying and desperate, appealed for clemency and mercy, especially on behalf of the five young children. They cried in unison. In German, now, their voices and tears went unheeded. We were then forced to stand against the wall. The children were crying and screaming, and the women were sobbing loudly. The lieutenant lined up his patrol, cum firing squad and sudden executioners with their weapons drawn. To our fevered, disbelieving minds, now stretched to the limit of human endurance, everything turned into a slow motion nightmare, as one would expect when one is looking into the business end of a German Luger and seven rifles. Finally: "Ready" . . . an eternity passed during that second . . . "Aim" . . . Suddenly another German officer came running out of the house, arms and hands wildly gesturing in the air, screaming "Stop! Stop! Stop! For god's sake stop! Stop now!" . . . and indeed the lieutenant and his men looked over to the screaming officer and slowly lowered their weapons.

Obviously this officer was the lieutenant's superior. (We later found out that he was a captain, and in charge of the German company quartered in this beautiful farm house.) The captains face was red with rage. Coatless, dressed in his shirt, he showed relief that he was able to avoid an unwarranted, disastrous execution of innocent and helpless women and children by a split second. His shoulders now slumped as if to indicate the passing of his alarm and tension. He turned to us with a sigh and asked us to sit on the grass and try to relax. He then turned to the overeager and potentially murderous lieutenant. After a long, disapproving glare at this man, supposedly the best that Germany's youth had to offer, he began to sternly lecture him in front of his own men. "In the German Army, yes the German Army", he repeated as if for emphasis, "we do not shoot women and children in cold blood. Lieutenant, you are dismissed for now. We will speak again later." He then dismissed all but one member of the patrol, a young private who by now looked totally bewildered . . . and pale.

Then the captain turned to us. He asked if we were alright. Without apologizing directly, his manner and body language spoke a thousand sympathetic and empathetic words. "I don't really know what to do now", he finally said with a sigh. "They don't teach this sort of thing at Officer's Infantry School." Pause. "I guess you can . . . no, you must leave now. As far as you are concerned this incident never happened. Do you know where to go?" he added rhetorically. "Do you need any food? My man here can get you some." "No thank you", the women replied in unison. They were understandably eager to leave. "At least some fruit . . .", he trailed off. Already guiding their children toward the exit, the women emotionally thanked the captain "for everything" and kept walking briskly as if out of the gates of hell. Once past the wall, which now felt no less threatening than on the inside, the women nevertheless breathed a deep sigh of relief, albeit for the moment only. In order to avoid attention and suspicion, my mother suggested that we make our way back to Brussels separately, regroup there, and try again some other day at some other location. When one of our Belgian friends heard about the Nazi lieutenant, the former mumbled under his breath "A Maquis sniper will get him soon enough." Our circle of friends in Brussels was diminishing. The Schloss family was able to leave by ship from Antwerp. They safely sailed to New York, and proceeded to Los Angeles. After the war, being restaurateurs by trade, they opened a bistro and catering business in Palm Springs. Mother would visit them many, many years later.

Back in our apartment in Brussels, the immensity of this aborted attempt and its near—death experience, plus the overall difficulty in illegally crossing borders under German control, had sunk in and landed with a heavy—but sobering—thud, my mother would admit much later. What unthinkable luck and good fortune we were granted. This could not be attempted again in an unplanned, impromptu way. Through her still-intact, but now somewhat jaded network of friends, mother urgently proceeded to search for a "guide" to assist in an attempted second border crossing into France. And she found one: "A seemingly very shrewd, young Jewish woman of Polish descent", in my mother's words. The young woman, according to the rumor, an ousted Polish Freedom Fighter, was extremely competent in her newly-found vocation. Money changed hands, and the crossing was a success. The French Resistance and the Poles, for now sharing a common enemy, formed an alliance with due speed and unity of purpose, and respective connections in the Resistance. We will hear about the French Resistance and the Maquis again and again as this book proceeds on its inevitable course into greater and graver danger. (The Maquis was the arm of the French resistance movement that operated primarily in the rural areas.)

CHAPTER 4

France

The Chameleon.

France had been invaded by the German Wehrmacht on May 17, 1940, one week after the conquest of Belgium. On June 17, 1940, Marshall Petain, at the request of the newly-formed Vichy-based collaborative government, negotiated an armistice with Germany. His request was granted on June 22, 1940. French troops officially laid down their arms, and in return approximately forty percent of the French nation, the Southern portion, was to remain unoccupied.

It was now July 11, 1941. The good news was that America had still not entered the war, holding out faint hope the Feibelmann family, reuniting in the port city of Marseilles, could yet escape continental Europe by sea. The bad news was that my mother and I were now on the French side of the border. The German Army, the *Waffen-SS*, and the Gestapo were swarming everywhere. No place to linger.

The plan was to take the train or a bus to Laon, although it would still be in the German-occupied part of France. The train sounded risky. The word on the street was that trains were frequently subject to routine inspections for identity cards, passports, and other papers by the French police, often supervised by the Gestapo. It was decided that a bus, motoring on the secondary roads, would be safer. Not necessarily so! Somewhat unexpectedly, and with a sudden stop, we realized that we had run into a checkpoint of the French police. They didn't look kindly on my mother's German passport and declared my mother and me—along with our fellow-refugee travel companions—to be prisoners of the Vichy government. We were told to remain on the bus under the guard of one of the policemen. The police then "escorted" us back towards the border, namely to Charleville where we spent two dreadful nights in a French jail, not knowing what the next day would bring: life or certain death? On the third morning, we were rather unceremoniously released by the officials of the jail. The trademark of the French Resistance was stamped all over in this unexpected release . . . and that was—once again—the good news. The bad news, however, was the difficult challenge ahead: the task of a second attempt to reach of the demarcation line between occupied and unoccupied France . . . and then cross it . . . and soon. This time help came from Lyon, south of the demarcation line dividing Vichy France (or Free France, as it was also called) and the occupied part of France. Lyon was later to be identified as one of the operation centers of the French Resistance. My mother was in contact with a classmate and good friend of her younger years, Edith, who married a French Jew, born and raised in Lyon by parents who were long-time French nationals. His name was Raff (Raphael) Kahn. By the time of the French capitulation, he had been elevated to the rank of Major in the French Army. When the French army disbanded, he returned to the family's textile business. The Kahns gave my mother only the surname of "a person of considerable authority" to see at the office of the Ministry of the Interior, Dijon Division. "Do not be frightened, nor intimidated, for things are not always as they appear," they told my mother. The next day, my mother—once again with me in tow—gathered all her courage and unity of purpose, and proceeded to the Ministry. At the reception desk, with its newly-found German coldness, officiousness, and work ethic rhythm, she carefully asked for this "person". It turned out to be a tall, severe-looking, French woman in a dark, very conservative and proper business suit, flashing the familiar and dreaded Nazi armband on her sleeve. My mother, her knees buckling, thought how is this possible? Is this a trap? The French woman asked my mother to please enter her office. Closing the door behind her just slightly, she quickly proceeded to give my mother the name of the Postmaster of the town of Sennecey le Grand. She instructed my mother not to write down the name until after she left the building. "Proceed to this little border town with care and see him . . . and only him", she continued. And, with that she bid us a hurried farewell. It turned out that the mystery woman was leading a double-life: By day a high-ranking French-Nazi official and apparent collaborator; by night, or whenever urgently necessary, a member of the Resistance. How's that for living dangerously? We never found out what happened to this brave soul because our Lyon friend and life-saving contact, the French Army Major, lost contact with her. Such matters sadly remained a mystery. She may have been shot by the Nazis the very next day; or she could have eventually "worked" her way westward to the coast, where she and her comrades would assist the Allied landings with great and highly productive success. C'est la guerre.

The next morning, mother and I journeyed to Sennecey and indeed located the Postmaster. He too acted hurriedly. He wanted to be quite certain that we were alone in his little post office. He reached behind him and tore off a piece of heavy, brown wrapping paper from its roll. The "sheet of paper" had no particular shape, no corners, nor straight edges. It looked haphazardly torn off. On it, he hand wrote the equivalent of a short safe conduct note (or paragraph), put his all-important postmaster's rubber stamp on it, and signed it. He told us to cross the Demarcation Line between the two Frances at the one and only nearby "border crossing" the very next day as punctually as possible between the hour of eleven o'clock and noon. Mother understood immediately. That was the time his Resistance "buddy" would be on guard . . . and once again, it worked! Increasingly, we owed a great debt of gratitude to the men and women of the French Resistance for their tireless work, always under pressure and in grave danger.

Once across "the line", we headed for Lyon, where a warm—and on my mother's part—grateful reunion with the Kahn family took place. We only stayed overnight, as we did not want to endanger their apparent, but tenuous security by our mere presence. We were now in a position to take the train to Marseilles and hopefully reunite with my father.

CHAPTER 5

La Republique Francaise

The Art of Collaboration

We were now in the "free" part of France. The date was July 19, 1941. Never skipping a beat—and since, after all, it was still early in the day—my mother inquired about its location and proceeded straight to the Sennecey Surete (the police station) to obtain a Safe Conduct document to travel in the unoccupied part of France, specifically to Marseilles. Purpose: emigration to the United States. It was granted the same day and without bureaucratic hurdles, on condition that my mother report to the Agency for Foreigners at the "Prefecture des Bouches du Rhone" immediately upon arrival in Marseille. Interestingly, it also gives permission to my mother to contact—by telephone—the chief of the Camp Des Milles, the "transit camp" at which my father remained interned. The camp, situated just south of Aix-en-Provence, was a short train ride away from central Marseilles.

After a quick phone call to distant relatives (through the Lowenberg side of the family) and dear friends in Marseilles, the Eichberg family, who were anxiously awaiting the call, my mother and I then proceeded to the train station and boarded the next train to the gritty port city on the Mediterranean. "Free" France, my mother quickly learned, was not so free. A *Commissariat* for Jewish Affairs was set up as early as late-March 1941 in Vichy. In May, Marshall Petain issued a radio broadcast approving collaboration with Hitler. The Gestapo was involved in everything. It was greatly feared—and despised—by the French population on this side of the Demarcation Line. Therefore, speed—and trying to operate "under the radar"—was the order of the day, everyday day, for Jewish refugees.

We arrived in Marseilles rather late in the day and were met at the train station by Otto and Herta Eichberg. Merchants by profession, they had left Germany soon after the Nazis came to power. They lived at 17 Rue des Phoceens, Marseille. At this point, they had not been bothered in any way by the Gestapo and/or by French officialdom. We stayed with them until suitable lodgings could be arranged. The Eichbergs would be of enormous help to us.

Priority One was to re-unite with my father, whom we had not seen for a year, and my grandfather at camp Des Milles, which my mother arranged with her usual efficiency. Mother and I were ecstatic. It was a tearful reunion. She brought food and other items not readily available in a Vichy camp. Beyond the physical effects of grief, worry, and the constant unknown and unpredictable, my father looked relatively well and continued to cling to the hope that a sea departure was possible . . . if only that United States quota number would come up. Not a chance! The quota number issued by the American Consulate in Stutgart, Germany, on August 31, was number 18397. (Exh.) He worked in the office of the camp, and his efficiency was welcomed by the camp commander, he told my mother. Mother continued to have some meager funds available. New funds, about $300, were sent to Marseille from a friend of my father who resided in New York City and a cousin who resided in Brunswick, New Jersey. (Exh.)

Mother and I took up residence in a small hotel recommended by the Eichbergs. It was located at 34 Allees Gambetta. The owner, a woman, (You guessed right!) was a member of the Resistance. She was a discreet, kind, helpful, compassionate, and trustworthy woman in whom we could confide. I attended school in Marseilles, Ecole Communale, for only a very short time. It was too risky, too dangerous, and did not fit the "below the radar" survival parameters. Mother and I continued our visits to Des Milles, bringing food, toiletries, and above all love and care to my father and grandfather. My mother realized that this would involve regular visits. My mother always had the strength and the ability to help the entire family, and where applicable, friends—and even strangers—as well. Due to these travel requirements, albeit short-range, my mother reluctantly requested—and promptly received an Identification Card from the Free French government, Central Division Marseille, on August 8, 1941, a month after we arrived in Marseille. (Exh.) By November of 1941 the office of the commissioner of the police department requested that my mother report every month to have her "papers" renewed and her status reviewed. (Exh.) In the meantime, the Nazis intensified the hunt for all European Jews running or hiding.

Simultaneous to declaring war on Japan after the Pearl Harbor attack, America also declared war against Germany on December 11, 1941. Hitler, who fashioned his career, national and international politics, and military actions, on the example of the great conquerors of history, had no intention of altering his *modus operandi.* However, Hitler had always hoped that America would not enter the war. In some corner of his twisted, evil brain, he began to realize that the war was lost at that very moment. The saner of his generals, the Wehrmacht generals, as opposed to the SS fanatics, came to that conclusion immediately.

Typically prioritizing the "War Against the Jews" as more important than the war against the allies, Hitler wasted no time in calling a conference to include those to whom the conduct of the "Final Solution" had been entrusted. Hitler was in a total frenzy. He wanted the conference to begin as soon as December 18th. However, the matter of the declaration of war on the United States—and vice versa—had to be presented to the Reichstag, at least as a matter of form. Hitler, therefore, reluctantly agreed to begin the conference on January 20, 1942. It was to be held at a large, luxurious house in Wannsee, the pleasant lakeside suburb of Berlin. The house was the former property of a Jewish "Berliner" family. I **strongly** believe that the Wannsee Conference represented the seminal turning-point in the conduct of the Final Solution. I further believe that the Conference illuminates—more than any other single element in the formation of the policy of the Final Solution of the Jewish Problem—the pervasive German mindset as clearly as Wannsee. In 2002, a friend asked me to read, and then write a book report on "The Wannsee Conference and the Final Solution", a new publication written by Mark Roseman. At this point of the narrative, I offer below excerpts from my report.

The Conference—and its Protocol—serves as an unambiguous definition of the Final Solution. It exemplified the Rhetoric of Extermination. It served as a set of strict directives taken from Hitler's writings (mainly "Mein Kampf"), his speeches and his activities from 1919 to 1933, and then on to 1941, the eve of the conference. According to Hitler, the order of battle was emigration/evacuation followed by deportation followed by elimination by means of a genocidal program! In other words, *all* were to die. (In that connection, Daniel Goldberg correctly calls German anti-Semitism a unique "eliminatory anti-Semitism".) Most of the men at the conference table subscribed to this mindset. The chairman of the conference was Reinhard Heydrich, head of the Nazi Security and Chief of the German Security Police. He reported directly to Himmler, arguably—along with Goering—the closest person to Hitler.

The background for the conference can be said to go back a few years. It can be traced to the Nazi government's ambiguous pressure on German Jews to emigrate. The German Jewish community's perceived failure and reluctance to do so erupted on *Kistallnacht,* November 9, 1938. Conclusion: A regime that could promote and sanction such a night of widespread horror could—and would—sanction any crime against humanity. Anti-Semitism became the badge ambitious Nazis would wear to legitimate their claims and demands, especially among the educated and the competent German bureaucrats. The mass shootings of men, women and children began before the era of the gas chamber and the crematorium. Detailed head counts were sent to Berlin, revealing perhaps for the first time the full horror of the unique fusion of annihilatory (sic) ideology and bureaucratic fastidiousness. A middle management for murder was evolving. By the Fall of 1941, the first experiments with cyanide were carried out at Auschwitz, albeit on Soviet POW's. More importantly, by this time a genocidal policy had become the order of the day, with enforcement demanded, top-down, from The Fueher, Goering and Heydrich. In the meantime, Himmler had put Eichmann in charge of the day-to-day handling of the Final Solution. Striking, too, was the army's new acceptance of anti-Jewish measures as essential in fighting against the Soviets. A link was established between anti-Bolshevism and anti-Semitism. Fall eased into winter, and in December 1941 the United States finally entered the war. To many in the top Nazi leadership—yes, including Hitler—it began to dawn that Germany may not win the war. Hitler had dreaded a world war and American participation. However, it now gave him a chance to blame the Jews for the world war against him and his nation. More than ever, he pounced on the opportunity to blame the Jews for the world war. He invoked the time-worn global Jewish conspiracy theory and resurrected his infamous "prophesy" regarding the Jews and a world war. He had blamed WWI—and Germany's humiliating defeat—on world Jewry. He prophesied to the Jews that if they ever caused world war again they would suffer extermination. Period! By this heinous formula, extermination of the Jews—without sentimentality—now became the necessary consequence of their own actions. The defining moment of clarity had arrived. All this occurred *immediately* after war had been declared against the U.S.A. A psychological threshold had been irrevocably crossed. The systematic killing of *all* European Jews must be accelerated now. Hence the urgent need for this conference.

The Wannsee Conference and Protocol would merely put *everyone* on the same page: Get with the program! . . . sabotage our policies or drag your feet at your own peril! The Final Solution—a euphemism for mass murder—was placed within the reach of all lower-level officials, legitimized by the full knowledge and acquiescence of Hitler's own radical anti-Semitic agenda. The few remaining tolerant or liberal-minded Germans were forced into line. The conference was merely disseminating conclusions arrived at elsewhere. The participants listened and nodded and drank cognac. Although Heydrich found it necessary to remind his guests that Goering and Himmler had specifically entrusted him—as their representative—with preparing the Final Solution, they "happily"—and with pleasure—accepted the basic party line. (Himmler had always said: "The Jewish question belongs to me".) Perhaps it is not so surprising that the young men around the table were already true believers, for whom racist nationalism was at the heart of their own philosophy. They were by and large confirmed Nazis and not just dutiful functionaries. They had joined the party in the nineteen-twenties and made anti-Semitism their life's work. For those few who didn't quite fit into this mold at first, it merely proved that opportunism, the desire for order, or simply not questioning the validity of the task could be sufficient reason for underwriting genocide, in other words, mass murder! There was total agreement on the assertion that the Jews' lesser qualities as human beings justified their extermination. The gap between the men in the field and the "desk murderers" disappeared. The key departments and ministries—especially those pertaining to the territories outside of Germany—had already been stuffed full of party men; little remained of a civil service ethos. It was at this time that Goebbels acknowledged in his diary that deportation of the Jews to the East was "in many cases synonymous with the death penalty." With breathtaking calmness chairman Heydrich—quoting from the protocol—observed that around 11,000,000 Jews would be affected by the final solution in the European countries under Germany's control or occupation, Germany's European allies, neutral countries (!), and those with which it was still at war prior to America's entry into the war. Heydrich, Eichmann and the Protocol were not given to overlooking the significant matters. For example: As the large majority of Jews is eliminated, a final remnant of survivors will likely remain, consisting of the most resistant elements. They will have to be dealt with appropriately, lest by natural selection they form the germ cell of a new Jewish revival and a "new experience in history." There was no debate at the Conference about any of this. A consensus, led by Buehler of the *Generalgouvernement*, who handled all affairs outside Germany proper, was only concerned, as the minutes show, and verbalized as such, that all this "be solved as quickly as possible."

How significant was the Conference in unleashing the tide of genocide that followed? Up to early March 1942 (barely two months after the conference) less than ten percent of the Holocaust's eventual Jewish victims had perished. But, the period from March 1942 through mid-February 1943 saw the extermination of more than half of all the Jews that were to be annihilated at the Nazi's hands. All tentativeness was gone. The era of interim measures, "provisional solutions" and "temporary relief" was now at an end. Significant expansion plans for crematoria and gas chambers at Auschwitz began immediately, as did a new wave of Western European Jews destined for Auschwitz.

Even labor scarcities would not materially alter Heydrich's lethal policies. The labor "problem" would not provide psychological reservations to the policy of genocide. Jewish matters were taken away from the Ministry of the Interior. [A note to those readers whose Holocaust education consists mainly of the film *Schindler's List*: Throughout 1942, there would still be some fluctuating balance between manpower needs and Project Genocide. Given the subtleness of the priorities, Himmler's interventions in the labor problem were constantly shifting. To him only the final goal mattered, in that the decisions were not about whether to kill or not, but simply about when and in what order to kill. Again, it is in this sense that the Conference captured the transition to a clear program of mass murder.]

A further note: At the time of the Conference, only 131,000 Jews remained in Germany proper. Estonia, in a congratulatory birthday dispatch to Hitler, declared itself free of Jews, or *Judenrein,* proud to be the first in the German Reich to reach that goal. (How about those Estonians?!!) Major Jewish populations, however, remained in Poland and the Ukraine, combined over five million. Another five million still lived in the U.S.S.R. Nearly a million remained in occupied and unoccupied France, whose full collaboration was taken for granted by the Nazis. Yet another million remained in Romania and White Russia. As we saw above, the authors of the Protocol had the chutzpah to include 330,000 Jews living in England and the handful in the neutral countries of Portugal, Sweden and Switzerland. These figures account for the aforementioned total of eleven million. This number was further defined as to Jewish adherence to *faith,* since some countries did not have a definition of the term "Jew" according to racial principals. Heydrich was assassinated in 1943 by the Czech resistance at the behest of the British. Nothing changed.

No wonder that life for Jewish refugees in France was getting more and more hazardous. The Gestapo became more active and more visible. They began to look for us at our little hotel. (The French call it *Pension*: room and meals) The owner of the pension was either tipped off or recognized them at the last minute by their car and long leather coats. She would come to us quickly and send us up to attic. She would tell the Gestapo that we no longer lived there. They did not believe her.

Simultaneously, life for my father and his fellow detainees became more difficult. Since Des Milles was designated as a "transit camp", the internees feared imminent deportation to "The East. At this point, my father's "friendship"—and a bribe—with the camp commander paid off. My father, in an arrangement between the two camp commanders, was transferred to Aubagne. The latter had the great advantage of being only a street car ride away from Marseilles. My father was deeply torn, for it meant leaving his father behind. However, the transfer meant being closer to my mother and me. My father also realized the possibility of a potential joint escape to a neutral country. Aubagne was a minimum security work camp. Once again, my father worked in the office, per recommendation by the last camp commander.

However, the situation for the Jews-on-the-run continued to tighten. Consuming concern and high anxiety became a part of everyday life. Rumors of deportations circulated. Before leaving one weekend to visit mother and me, shortly after his arrival at Aubagne, the camp commander, whom my father had befriended, whispered in his ear not to return from his weekend pass. Upon his arrival in Marseilles, my father told my mother. She understood immediately, telling him by all means not to return. By this time my mother had a new contact in the countryside and she would take him there at once. However, my father was not convinced, and postponed his decision until the following day, Sunday. As the following morning went on, my father told my mother that he decided to return to the camp. This Germanic, disciplined, surviving veteran of World War One was not about to go A.W.O.L. My mother was now in total shock and disbelief. She was in tears. To her this was beyond belief and all reason. She clamored and pleaded. She "guaranteed" him that the temporary escape to the countryside estate of her friend would succeed. "We have the means to go on from there," she told him. To no avail. He returned to Aubagne, only to find out that he had been ordered back to Des Milles.

During the following week, my father was transferred to the much larger camp at Drancy. From there he—along with 990 "prisoners"—was shipped out by means of the ubiquitous cattle car on Transport Number 19 on August 14, 1942. Destination: Auschwitz. 875 prisoners were alive upon arrival.

(Exh.) According to eye witnesses, the new arrivals were immediately marched to the gas chamber . . . where they were promptly murdered by the Nazis. The Germans kept good records. At the conclusion of their triumphantly successful victory, they planned to build a museum dedicated to an extinct race. Of course, in the desperation of the moment, the circumstances and facts were not quite so clear. On August 8, 1942, less than a week before the actual deportation from Drancy, my mother sent a telegram to my father at Camp Des Milles, hoping to get some clarification and/or further information. She did not know that he was no longer there. The telegraph was intercepted by the authorities at Des Milles, and finally on the August 13th, she received the following reply: 'The Addressee has left without leaving a forwarding address.' (Exh.) Also, the reports of the above-mentioned eye witnesses came much later, as did the German's meticulous "bill of lading". Therefore, my mother was able to continue to cling to the smallest ray of hope that my father may have miraculously survived. Later, when the death camps were at long last liberated by the Allies, mass confusion reigned. The freed inmates spread out in all directions, mostly westward of course, where Displaced Persons camps were set up by the Allies, augmented by various international and local aid agencies, including the Red Cross. We—including my father's sister in London—eagerly inquired and awaited word that my father was, or had passed through one of these camps. It was a long shot . . . and we all knew it. As the Displaced Persons camps emptied and the drifting survivors found their destinations, it became all too clear that my father did not survive Auschwitz. Official notification came only later, as an official search and research was established for this purpose in Paris. Mother received a letter from this organization (S.E.R.) after we had already settled in New York, dated February 20, 1947, attesting to the deportation from Drancy to Auschwitz, complete with date, etc., and further advising my mother, once again, that father's name could not be found on list of survivors. (Exh.) In October of 1947, my mother received an attest from the new Republique Francaise's Ministry of Combatants and War Victims posthumously awarding my father a "Certificate of Honor for Valor—to which the recipient is rightfully entitled."

CHAPTER 6

Narrow Escape

The Hour of Darkness.

Marseilles, August 1942. Shortly after my dear father was deported, a warning was relayed to my mother by the lady who owned and operated "our" little hotel that the Gestapo had further increased their numbers and the intensity of their searches. We were now "officially" on their list. They would specifically be looking for us. It was high time to get out of town. The French Vichy government special police was already making daily inquiries. The pension keeper told them that we had been gone for quite some time. Checked out. No forwarding address. That was not good enough for the Gestapo, and they paid the pension a visit the very next day. The owner told them the same story. Of course, we were still in the building, hiding in the attic, whereupon the Gestapo took all our belongings. The Gestapo discovered the pension owner's Resistance membership about three months later, dragged her out into the street, and shot her on the spot as an example to the neighbors, who had gathered in the street, of what happens to "traitors", so mother was later told by a reliable source. My mother contacted her friend at the aforementioned farm. We went there immediately. The farm was near Marseille, easily accessible by streetcar. She was a somewhat mysterious woman. Unbeknownst to my mother and to her village neighbors and the community, she was a Jewish woman of German birth, married to a Gentile Frenchman long before the war. She spoke French perfectly. He was serving in a "branch" of the theoretically disbanded French Army in North Africa. DeGaulle ran a controversial secret operation there under British protection. The most important part of my mother's friend's mysterious life and demeanor: she carried a diplomatic pouch and made regular visits to Switzerland! We would stay with her for a total of ten days.

Here is the plan that evolved during that period with the aid of people already mentioned in previous chapters. First, mother needed money. Our host went to Switzerland to pick-up a heavy gold bracelet and some gold coins, kept with relatives since 1938. The bracelet was made especially for a purpose such as this. Simultaneously, the previously-mentioned Eichbergs approached a friend in Marseille. He was a policeman and a member of the Resistance. He obtained a false/forged French passport: false names, false "everything" . . . and his services were gratis! This wonderful man just wanted to help people in mortal danger and extreme circumstances and do his little share to thwart the Nazis, the occupiers of his country, his beloved land. The carrier of the passport, my mother, would be from Strasbourg in the French territory of Alsace, a part of France that over the millennium was ruled by France and Germany according to the winds of war so common in Europe. The inhabitants of Alsace, therefore speak French and/or German along with a dialect that is a mixture of the two languages. This had to be done because my mother spoke very little French.

It is no hyperbole to say that the French Resistance did in fact save our lives. During and after the invasion at the Normandy beaches, the Allied Armies would later learn of the huge value of the Resistance operating behind enemy lines. Throughout the nearly six years of war, the Resistance would pay a heavy price for their operations. And so would the general French population in the vicinity of their acts of sabotage. An entire village—men, women and children—would be wiped out in reprisal for a blown-up German Army truck, or interrupting rail service, or severed telephone lines, etc. etc. Vive la Resistance! Yes, we still eat French Fries, not Victory Fries, as I imagine the dwindling few American survivors of the Normandy Invasion of 1944 do as well.

We left the farm and entrained at Marseille, bound for Lyon still in the unoccupied part of France. Now, every step, every move had the potential of grave risk and fatal danger. My mother, getting her timing just right, decided not to take seats in the passenger cars, but rather join a long line of passengers waiting a for table in the dining car. And surely, at one of the train's stops the French police boarded and "worked" the passenger cars, checking IDs. Mother was right again. The border police did seem a bit more relaxed in asking for papers and generally screening the people on the dining car line. By this time, I spoke French quite well. In their general presence on the train, my mother asked me to be especially vocal. In Lyon, everything was prearranged. In order not to draw attention to ourselves and thereby endanger the aforementioned Kahn family, we stayed at a small inn on the outskirts of Lyon. Need I say that once again the owner of the inn was a member of the Resistance? Rafael "Raff" Kahn, a French citizen born in the Alsace and a former Major in the now disbanded French Army, had made arrangements for a guide to illegally take us across the Swiss border. May I add here that the Major and his entire local family, including his parents, would survive the war in Lyon.

As for our escape to Switzerland, just when everything was proceeding like clockwork, there suddenly was a delay. My mother developed an infection on her foot and could not walk. She managed to see a doctor who performed a minor procedure. However, the delay stretched into two valuable weeks. Finally, early on a rainy, stormy day, after an urgent wake-up call from our guide, Mother and I finally left Lyon on a moment's notice. We boarded a train that would take us through the lovely, lush countryside of occupied France. Destination: Annemasse, on the Swiss border. Our guide was traveling separately on the same train. He had been paid in advance in Lyon. Also somewhere on that train was a gentleman by the name of Willy Rosen, a bachelor and friend of my parents from Brussels days. He, like so many refugees, was penniless. My mother financed his expenses, including the guide's fee. He would turn out to be extremely helpful during the hazardous border crossing. After detraining, our guide took mother and me to a hut in the forest to await nightfall. He returned to town to pick up Willy. Shortly thereafter, he materialized once again with the other members of our crossing party: A Dutch family consisting of parents and three small children. The guide had purposely waited for a wet, nasty day and night. In the driving, soaking rain the German border guards tended to stay in their narrow little huts. Their dogs were less likely to pick up our scent. Walking through the now-drenched forest and the wet leaves on the ground made far less noise than on a dry forest floor. At about nine o'clock, as we waited for complete darkness, we were suddenly attacked by two or three French-speaking men. They said that they were members of the plain-clothes French police. But, of course they weren't. They robbed our pathetic little group of refugees of all valuables: watches, jewelry, and money. The Dutch family had a lot of money and jewelry on their persons. It was gone. Except for a few French Francs and loose coins, my mother had characteristically made the necessary precautions. She had sewn valuables into the base of her small suitcase . . . and the gold coins into her corset. These thugs got nothing, zero, zilch! It was soon apparent that our "brave" attackers were, of course, accomplices of the guide, as was later confirmed through the always-present grape vine of poor souls that preceded and followed us at this venue. After letting us rest a bit after this chilling, terrifying experience, the innocent—and appalled-acting guide brought us through the forest TO the border, not ACROSS the border. He bid us a hearty farewell and good luck. 'Just proceed in this general direction and you'll have no problem', were his parting words. Well, that was a bit of a shock to us. However, there was no time to commiserate amongst each other. Yes, everything would now be far more difficult. But our mission was clear: go now, last chance, just do it, survive . . .!

The Swiss-French border consisted of three rows of barbed wire on the French side, a broad strip of no-man's land divided by a stream, and beyond another three rows of barbed wire on the Swiss side: not exactly an easy obstacle to traverse under any conditions, but especially not in the necessary darkness and drenching rain. My mother later told me that visibility was so poor that she had trouble seeing me at three paces. The Dutch dad was busy helping his family. Willy helped mother and me. At times, the two men jumped in wherever assistance was needed. Clothes were soaked and torn, a little blood drawn here and there . . . and we were cold. We struggled forward . . . or what we hoped was forward. It was a huge test of strength of will, stamina, and survival instinct.

About midnight, worn-out, tired, wet, bones aching to the core, we stopped in the belief that we had indeed crossed the border and were standing on Swiss soil. But, were we really in Switzerland? Did we get disoriented in the dark and in the rain? Did fatigue and exhaustion play its potentially deadly role? We couldn't see the hand in front of our faces. Did we erroneously circle back and were we in fact standing on French ground, not Swiss? Yet, we were at a point of no return. Our weary party dragged itself through the forest until we arrived at a gated house. The gate was locked. Willy climbed over the gate, and in the dark of night thought that he saw two cars in the driveway with Swiss license plates. Nevertheless, he reluctantly awakened the homeowner in order to confirm that the house was indeed within Swiss borders. He did not mention that he was part of a group of seven refugees. The answer was in the affirmative. The homeowner, somewhat ill-humored due to his early wake-up call, acknowledged that he was indeed on Swiss soil and let him out through the locked front gate.

We proceeded down a dirt road, and collapsed under a tree which gave us a little shelter as the rain slowed. Now, there was no alternative to awaiting daybreak . . . and finally it came. The rain had stopped now. The road was deserted. We later learned that the Swiss had only a few weeks earlier reversed their unconscionable policy/procedure of routinely and mercilessly turning back refugees at the borders, which had of course been a death sentence.

It was September 16, 1942.

CHAPTER 7

Switzerland

Safe Harbor in the Storm.

Finally, shortly before seven o'clock, mother saw a bicycle approaching in the distance. As it came closer, mother realized that it was a Swiss policeman. Good fortune or ill? My mother and I—and our huddled companions—would find out in a minute or two. It was indeed a local Swiss policeman on his way to work. He stopped, got off his bicycle and wondered aloud where we had come from. He hardly began to question us when the story of our border crossing just rolled off everyone's tongue showing the release from fear and anxiety, even in the face of an uncertain future. The French-speaking policeman responded in a positive manner. He would, of course, have to take us to his police station, but all in due time. But, for the moment, he observed, "you all look tired, wet, and hungry. So, let's go back to my house first". This was our first indication that the general Swiss population would be friendly to refugees, most importantly to Jews. Of course, in the French-speaking part of Switzerland, they would be far more easy-going than in the German-speaking (read: Germanic) part. At his house, he insisted to serve breakfast. His daughter went out to get fresh rolls and Danish pastry. His wife made hot coffee to warm us up. The policeman, surrounded by his family, asked every member of the group to tell his story about the events that preceded the border crossing and life under the Nazis in general. When my mother told them our story, tears welled up in their eyes. My mother later told me "after almost ten years, I felt for the first time that I was once again being treated as a worthy and complete human being." However, this emotional and sweet *Kaffeeklatsch*—this friendly, almost loving reception—had to end.

The policeman escorted us to the local police station. His colleagues were extremely friendly as well. His superior, a caring and mild-mannered man, now took over the interrogation. He asked my mother whether we had any friends or relations in Geneva. She answered, yes, the Muehlstein family. Mother had never met them. They were friends of the aforementioned Lowenberg family. Dorothy Lowenberg was my father's sister. "You mean the department store Muehlsteins?" inquired the Police Superintendent . . . "everyone in Geneva knows them." He called the Muehlsteins at once, telling them that Leon Feibelmann's wife and seven-year old son were sitting in his police station, having escaped Nazi-occupied France. They said that they would come to pick us up at once, and would assume all responsibilities for "adopting" the refugee family. The Police Superintendent was, of course delighted. It meant less work for him, less paper work, no need to find an interim solution for my mother and me . . . but, much to his credit, there was also the humanitarian angle. The Muehlsteins had two daughters, aged eighteen and twenty, and lived in a large, luxurious apartment, more than sufficient in size to house mother and me. The understanding was that we would live with them for an open-ended period of time, depending on the progress of the war. After four weeks of rest and recuperation and acclimatization, I was even registered to begin school. However, on the very next day a letter arrived from the Swiss authorities summoning my mother and me to a "collecting point" near Geneva enroute to Bueren-an-der-Aare, a Swiss refugee camp. Bueren was—and still is—a village hard to find on the map. It was in the vicinity of Bern, the Swiss capital.

The pleasantries ended when it came to the Swiss government. The government was traditionally anti-Semitic, especially Herr Rotermund, the sitting President of the Confederation of Switzerland. In late August 1942, the pressure to give Jews asylum in Switzerland came from the Swiss *people*! . . . not the government. Of course, mother and I remained thankful and grateful to have found a safe haven in Switzerland. That alone, however, does not prevent me from saying that Bueren was a desolate, primitive, "nasty" camp . . . just a foul place in general. It smelled of "Angst." The Swiss authorities, obsessively bureaucratic and fear-mongering, seemed to be rubbing the refugees' noses in the sad fact that their old way of life had vanished, perhaps forever. They seemed to traffic in an almost consuming spirit of official *Schadenfreude* especially reserved for their Jewish wards, of course. It infiltrated their already sinister psyche like a captivating obsession.

Bueren was a camp hastily built to house Polish anti-Nazi soldiers and freedom fighters, who had likewise escaped to Switzerland. They were transferred to make room for the growing number of civilian refugees. The camp was virtually empty when mother and I and fellow refugees arrived. The grounds of the camp were a field of deep mud, in parts covered by wooden planks to create "sidewalks". Bedding consisted of straw and sheets. We lived out of suitcases. There was running water in the barracks, but no toilets; latrines were available in a separate nearby barrack. A very primitive dining area was present in each barrack. The food, cooked by internees, had to be picked up in the central kitchen. Men and women were separated, including married couples. Children under the age of twelve stayed with their mothers. On the positive side, the food was very good and plentiful. This can be said about all the camps throughout Switzerland. Also, the camp was temporarily commanded by a Swiss Brigadier General . . . a wonderful man in every aspect, who took great pride in taking care of his sorry new flock as best he could with the materiel he had inherited. He would be replaced only too soon. There were two nurses to tend to sick and/or injured. A daycare center was provided for the children; two Swiss ladies ran it. Soon, the kitchen—along with the in-barracks eating areas—was discontinued. The meals were now brought in by a sub-contracted, local, offsite "restaurant". A large common dining hall was created. The owners of the restaurant also operated a canteen at the camp, where the internees could buy non-rationed food items to augment the meals if they felt so inclined. It was open for a few hours every afternoon. My mother—as always not letting any grass grow under her feet—and a Jewish French woman ran the canteen. They were compensated by the owners of the canteen. Except for the physical lack of even the minimal comforts of the barracks, things went along quite well. New internees trickled in from all the Nazi-occupied territories, and included anti-Nazi newspaper journalists and editors, clergy (especially Catholic dissenters), members of a small group of German anti-Nazi bureaucrats, Allied flyers whose planes had been shot down but were able to reach and cross the Swiss border, and—temporarily—some new Polish freedom fighters. Things were to change for the worse overnight, when the Swiss military man was ordered back to his division, to be replaced by Herr Mayer, a typically anti-Semitic bastard. After the war, he would be tried and convicted for mistreating refugees, receiving a five-year prison term. Give some credit to the Swiss judicial system!

My mother, not trusting the immediate future, decided on another course: separation.

She decided that these camps were no place for a child, namely me. With her characteristically remarkable and unique resourcefulness, she contacted a Swiss aunt of my father—aunt Martha, a sister of my paternal grandmother (maiden name Rosenthal)—to float the idea of taking me out of camp life, and letting me grow up in a family atmosphere (rather than communal) and benefit from regular schooling. Aunt Martha, a widow, told my mother that she herself lived under meager circumstances in a tiny, plain apartment in a small border village on the Rhine River. Although she knew our family well—and worried about the fate of her sister and, of course, my father—she would be unable to take anyone in. However, she added, that she was truly delighted that we had made it to the safety of Switzerland and again voiced deep concern about my father. But, then came the good news. She had a sister-in-law, she said, in the city of St. Gallen, named Selma Neuburger. The Neuburgers, she continued, were wealthy, naturalized Swiss citizens, living a patrician life-style in a large, luxurious home with their two Swiss-born sons. My mother and father had met the Neuburgers only once at a family wedding in Zurich in 1937. Aunt Martha said that she would immediately contact the Neuburgers by telephone. She called back only a short time later to tell my mother that the reply was an unhesitating "Yes".

CHAPTER 8

Katie's Choice

Entre'acte

My mother's decision to place her one and only child, now just approaching his eighth birthday, in the care of a foster family, was in many ways extraordinary. She based her decision on strictly obvious observations and expectations. Determination was driving a woman of character and humanity to this most practical and remarkable act. On the other hand, I was frightened and anxious. I cried and begged my mother to let me stay with her. Yet, an important part of me must have said: This unique woman's persistence, resourcefulness and love have brought us to this point and have in all likelihood saved our lives. How can I possibly be as undisciplined and ungrateful as to oppose her wishes now? You, dear reader, may translate that into the age-appropriate thinking process and language of a child. The nature of Camp Bueren had much to do with her decisive action. It was just plain unpleasant in every way, as previously described. The first indication that her instincts were right was the length of time—contrary to the concept of a temporary transient facility—mother and I had to stay in Bueren.

I left on January 24, 1943.

Mother stayed in Bueren. For mother and the other refuges at Bueren, the long harsh winter had begun. The huge weight of the sad, difficult events before, during and immediately after my father's deportation, the dangers of Marseille, the ever-present specter of the GESTAPO, the perilous trip across France, the horrific border crossings and their peripheral "theater", and the unknown present and future had all taken a physical toll on mother. She kept balancing and juggling all these and the new balls in the air, putting on a strong front . . . until I had left. Then, she more or less collapsed with severe bronchitis.

1938

CHAPTER 9

St. Gallen and the Neuburger Family

"What Do I Have To Do To Make You Love Me?"
—Sir Elton John

I entertained the idea of naming the previous chapter "Sophie's Choice", for I am absolutely certain that my mother thought only of the positive side of separation, convinced that her decision would be advantageous for me, now and in the foreseeable future. I cannot remember any immediate outburst of protest on my part: no resounding outcries of, say, 'I don't want to go! I'm not going to go!', all in the public arena of a camp barracks. Numbness is difficult to verbalize. I was accustomed to my mother making correct decisions. After all, in saving her own life, she saved mine. Yet, this decision was a two-edged sword. Was it rescue from less-than-pleasant internment or was it "abandonment" yet again. To the mind of a seven-year old child my dear father's sudden departure seemed like an act of abandonment. And now, it struck again! This decision would alter my life forever, consciously and sub-consciously. Many, many eons later—in adult life—years of analysis on the Freudian couch and the ensuing life-long treatment made only a dent in this conundrum. You, dear reader, will have to draw your own conclusions. One thing is clear to me: This remarkable woman—this serious, sensitive person of substance, my dearest mother—had only the very best of intentions. If there were serious doubts in her mind she neither exhibited them, nor verbalized them. Nor was she demonstratively aware of my torn, tortured thoughts and fears . . . neither then nor now.

After a tearful goodbye, both at the camp and at the small railway station of Bueren, I was suddenly alone, with a small suitcase and a name tag around my neck, sitting on a Swiss train. One more goodbye wave and the train left with characteristic Swiss punctuality. I feared the unknown future with strangers. I was—perhaps—even more nervous about changing trains in Bern. Approximately three and half hours later, I arrived in the city of St. Gallen in Northeastern Switzerland, a city of 60,000 inhabitants in the German-speaking part of the country. It was a typically rainy, cold late January afternoon. It would be dark soon. I detrained and just stood there on that platform and looked about. An impressive, well dressed, tall lady, who easily could have been my grandmother walked toward me. "Ernstly"?, she inquired. Then, seeing my name tag, she gave me a hug. She being so tall and me being so short, it was a somewhat awkward hug, the kind of brief hug you might give to an adult relative or friend. Albeit, I had at that moment in time met my foster mother, Selma Neuburger, age 59. She would be a great influence in my life for the next several years. It was two weeks past my eighth birthday.

During the war, the Swiss government appropriated most private automobiles. This, at least theoretically, saved gasoline, plus the Swiss Army needed sedan-type vehicles. So, we walked to what was to be my new home. It was a slow, mostly uphill walk in the rain. Conversation was not exactly spontaneous: 'Did I have a good trip? Did the change of trains go smoothly?' How was my mother? etc., etc . . . However, my new Aunt Selma did assure me that my mother would be able to visit me (us) soon. Nevertheless, I was tired and emotionally drained. Finally, we arrived at "Number 40." I could see, even through the rain and the mist and the darkening sky, that this was a stately home in a fine neighborhood situated on the steep slope of a hill above the city. As one of the heavy and beautiful wooden twin doors swung open into a large marble-floor entry area, a new life was about to begin for me. I immediately noticed the large, luxurious rooms, filled with art work and flowers, the high ceilings, huge windows and balconies. Our first act was to call my mother and tell her that I had arrived safely. She seemed relieved. Then, I was graciously offered a snack, as dinner would still be about two hours hence. At that time, I would meet the rest of the family, Aunt Selma's husband and their two sons. She warmly reiterated that I call her Aunt Selma and suggested that I call her husband Uncle David . . . perfectly reasonable, I thought. In the large kitchen, I met Hedi the cook/housekeeper, a sturdy young woman with rosy cheeks who grew up on a family farm in the nearby Canton of Appenzell. Her voice and body language immediately gave her away: She could only be warm, kind, helpful and caring. My first impression turned out to be totally true.

The former cook and housekeeper was a German national, who had lived in Switzerland, in service to the Neuburgers, for many, many years. However, shortly after the start of the war, the Swiss parliament passed a law stating that German-nationals could not work as servants to Jews! As dinner time drew nearer, I was about to meet the rest of the Neuburger clan. David Neuburger, age 64, ill with coronary disease, was the founder and owner of a successful ladies wear manufacturing business. He went to the office for a few hours on days when his health permitted. The younger of the two sons, Hanns, age 20, was forced to take over the everyday running of the business, due to his father's ill health. After graduating high school two years earlier, he was sent to Basel for a short apprenticeship, and at barely nineteen returned to head-up the day-to-day management of his father's business. Walter, one year older than Hanns, was home on winter break from the University of Geneva and his intermittent military service. He was scheduled to graduate that year and begin his doctoral program in pharmacology at the University of Bern.

This "new uncle", Uncle David, and this twenty year old business executive arrived punctually, as predicted. Brother Walter arrived a few minutes later. My first impression of Uncle David, a man of medium/average build, but now somewhat bent over due to his illness, was very positive: A welcoming glint in his eyes, a soothing man's voice, and a non-threatening and intelligent demeanor. Hanns was young man with prematurely serious responsibilities, which his bright smile belied. He seemed open, humorous, and on the same page with his parents in this venture—if all went well initially—to raise this "kid" for an unknown, open-ended period of time. "You'll be my roommate, buddy . . . so, don't worry about a thing." Not bad, I thought. This sleeping arrangement, this stroke of good fortune, was the result of Walter volunteering to sleep in the adjoining bedroom for the first few nights so I wouldn't be alone. And that—I would learn as time passed—was the quintessential Walter: student, intellectual, concerned, warm, generous, daredevil, military man, ladies' man, always living on the edge a bit . . . never indifferent to life, or people.

I was very tired. Nevertheless, dinner passed rather smoothly. Shy, and by no means at ease, I spoke when I was spoken to. Questions mainly revolved around foods I liked to eat. Hanns still likes to tell the story about that first evening. He recalls that I was asked whether or not I liked asparagus, the vegetable of the evening meal. Without skipping a beat, it seems that I answered "Yes, but only the tips". A knowing smile crossed his father's lips, Hanns added. We are not so sure about Aunt Selma's reaction. (I'll leave out the story about the baked chicken. But, Hanns, my dear, dear friend, you can fill in the blanks when you read this book.) All these pleasantries aside, Aunt Selma announced that it was finally bedtime for little Ernstly. After my subdued, polite "goodnight" to the gentlemen, she took me upstairs to the bedroom portion of the house . . . and indeed I would not have to sleep alone. The large bedroom with two twin beds separated by a night table, was since the days of their youth shared by Hanns and Walter. My new room mate, Hanns, I soon learned, was at the business at seven o'clock every morning, six days a week. He therefore retired early; but not this early. I undressed, washed up, brushed my teeth. Tired and exhausted I slumped into the bed like a rock. Aunt Selma said goodnight, kissed me on the forehead, turned off the light and went back downstairs. But, sleep would not come. I looked around the large, dark room with its high ceiling and began to sob. Emotionally alone in the world, I missed my mother to an indescribable degree. As my sobbing went on and on, only the housekeeper Hedi, having completed her kitchen chores for the night, heard me in her room on the floor above. She came down to comfort me. It worked. I finally fell asleep, only to awaken when roommate Hanns arose in the morning. "It's very early; go back to sleep; we'll talk later", he said. What I recall as about two hours later, say 8:30, Aunt Selma came into the room. Her manner gentle and reassuring, she very sweetly told me that it was time for breakfast. I should just brush my teeth and hair, and come next door for breakfast in my little robe. It was then, on the very first morning, that I learned that breakfast—continental, of course, with perhaps a soft-boiled egg—was a very important meal in the Neuburger household. The breakfast room was a bright room between the two main bedrooms. It had a large balcony. All three rooms faced south, important in a climate that left much to be desired. Hedi brought up breakfast from the kitchen.

Then Uncle David entered the breakfast room . . . also in his robe. It was made of navy silk, monogrammed, almost sartorial. The morning sunshine suddenly seemed a bit brighter. He looked better, refreshed by a night's sleep. He ate his fresh, just-delivered, baked-that-very-morning roll covered with butter (a luxury item indeed during the war's rationing) and dark bing cherry marmalade with gusto. He liked strong coffee. When Aunt Selma learned that the *one* thing that I didn't like was milk, a glass of chocolate milk was quickly substituted. After breakfast Uncle David took me out onto the balcony. The weather had changed overnight. Clear, sunny, brisk, I could see the view from "Number 40" for the first time. It was breathtaking. The city below us was situated in an East-West oriented valley. Across the valley was a large hill of about the same size and height we were standing on. It blocked out the rolling foothills of the Alpstein mountain range. But, the Alpstein massif, including its highest peak, the snow-covered Mount Saentis was clearly visible. Uncle David, although he had seen and admired this view a thousand times before was still impressed with it. In retrospect, I felt that somehow it symbolized his life. A poor immigrant orphan, he picked himself up by his bootstraps, became a Swiss citizen, worked hard and smart, and built a marvelous life for himself and his family. He loved this house, this home, which he built and completed in 1924. It would remain the family residence to this day (2010). That very morning a love affair began between a young boy and grandfatherly gentleman. Twenty-four hours ago they didn't even know each other.

Aunt Selma joined us with a "you had better get dressed now, young man . . . and perhaps we'll go downtown and buy you some new clothes." And so we did. After our shopping trip Aunt Selma suggested that I write to my mother in Bueren. I was closing in on the end of the first twenty-four hours in the life of a foster child. It was January 25, 1943. No one would have ever guessed that a relationship with the Neuburger family was forming, a relationship that is still happily in progress as of this writing.

CHAPTER 10

The Correspondence

The Vagaries of Human Frailty and Emotion.

My letter referred to at the end of the previous chapter is the first in a string of letters from Aunt Selma and me to my Mother. This correspondence was found among my mother's "stuff" after I began writing her memoirs. My mother keeps everything.

Regrettably, her replies to these letters were not preserved. Nevertheless, these letters illuminate the entire relationship with the Neuburger family from day one. We consider this relationship to be of utmost importance in all our lives.

The letter is dated January 25, 1943, one day after my arrival in St. Gallen on the previous day, January 24, 1943. I encourage my mother to ask for leave and visit me in St. Gallen, adding "Write as soon as possible." One thousand kisses, Your "Ernest."

We had changed my name from Ernst to "Ernest" in the French-speaking countries of Belgium and France and during our brief stay in Geneva. It would soon revert to Ernst in the German-speaking part of Switzerland. Only later, upon our emigration to the U.S.A., was it officially changed to Ernest. The correspondence follows in translation.

Aunt Selma waited a day and then added her own letter. The two letters were placed into one envelope and mailed on the 26th. Aunt Selma acknowledges that I arrived safely, as per previous telephone conversation, and that "they" (us/*wir*) already find the arrangement a very happy one. He's really a "cute kid", she writes, and after the passage of just these few days, we believe that he too will be satisfied with this arrangement. "Today, he is already in a brighter mood, whereas yesterday he was still homesick for his mother. Our housekeeper, Hedi, also likes him and handles him beautifully. He seems very much drawn to her. Importantly, our two sons took him into their hearts almost at once and my dear husband [hereafter referred to as Uncle David] beams with joy every time he sees the little guy. For an eight-year-old, he speaks so rationally, and reasonably and sensibly, as he correctly observes his new surroundings." The letter ends (1) with wishes that my mother's health improves, (2) that they are going to delay my start in school in order to enjoy a few days of leisure and "freedom" and (3) ends with most cordial salutations. [Author's note: Not bad for the first twenty-four hours . . . right? Are social skills—at any age—in fact survival skills, or perhaps a form of adaptation?]

Four days later, I write again, acknowledging my mother's reply with greatest of joy. I report that (1) Aunt Selma has registered me for school earlier today. In the age-appropriate third grade . . . and that I am not looking forward to school; (2) "they" bought me a very nice new suit, which I'm wearing right now; (3) I'm writing this letter while sitting in the kitchen with Miss Hedi (The kitchen was to become one of my favorite hangouts.); (4) that earlier in the afternoon, Hanns and Walter took me for a walk, as the weather is very nice, considering that it is mid-winter. I close with regards to all in mother's barrack and one million kisses.

To my one-page letter, Aunt Selma adds a two-pager. She cordially acknowledges mother's reply. She expresses satisfaction that mother has finally been transferred to the camp's infirmary, where she can hopefully benefit from the uniformly warm room temperature and bed rest. Additionally, she informs mother that she will talk to the camp commander as to what further action can be taken to assure mother's full recovery. Thoughtfully, she adds: "if that is agreeable to you"—a nod to the petty Swiss bureaucracy and an attempt not to get mother into any difficulties. She then confirms my starting school, telling my mother that it consists of only two hours, six days a week—and that she looks forward to the benefit of my beginning to make some friendships. She continues in saying that "in less than a week in the Neuburger household, the boy has become our dearest darling." She says that she regrets that mother cannot hear me talk about our war experiences, which she deems extraordinary. "At only the tender age of eight, he has an amazing talent to tell your—and his—story with unusual insight. Well, G-d willing, you can visit us soon and participate." For the first time, in this letter, Aunt Selma addresses mother as Mrs. Kate, rather than Mrs. Feibelmann.

I guess in order not to raise mother's hopes too much, she tells mother in a low-keyed manner that she and her husband have used some of their networking capabilities in an effort to have mother permanently released from the refugee camp on the grounds of her health, or at least transferred to a camp closer to St. Gallen.

Aunt Selma then reports that after a few nights their older son, Walter, returned to the bedroom that he and his brother shared since their earliest childhood, while I slept in the adjoining bedroom, perfectly happy and sleeping well. However, she continues, in about a fortnight Son Number Two, Hanns, "will have to report to military duty, an opportunity for Ernst to move back in with Walter, which Ernst is already looking forward to." (Note: Could any family be more sensitive, thoughtful and accommodating to total strangers?)

"Ernst also likes the food here", she continued. (Note: . . . and why not? Aunt Selma was an excellent cook and taught her help well. Meals were often of the gourmet variety even during the war and its more than adequate food rationing system. After the war, she really spread her culinary wings, only to improve and improve as I remember from my teenage years and my frequent all-summer visits. As the nuclear family grew, there was, after all, a reputation to uphold. My mother had many of Aunt Selma's recipes, and lovingly handed them down to my wife, Harriet. But, I'm getting ahead of myself: So back to the letters.) Aunt Selma proceeds to report the theme of the earlier letter, as to how pleased the family is in regard to the quick bonding with housekeeper/cook Hedi, and how much love she has to give. With Uncle David quite ill, and Aunt Selma needing to look to his needs as well, a "babysitter" became an important issue. She continues "and Ernst in turn helps by setting the table (note: quite formal) and—in fact—never forgets a single item."

She then turns to the subject of school and the beneficial fact that I spoke French and German. To fit in, the learning of the Swiss-German dialect—totally distinct from the conventional German—now has top priority. It seems that once again the housekeeper is in the forefront of this project, although the entire family is involved, she adds. "By the time you, Ms. Kate, come to visit, he will be able to greet you in proper *Schwitzerduetsch* (Swiss-German). In the meantime, he has the opportunity to use his knowledge of French with our sons." She concludes this long, unusually kind letter with the expression of get-well greetings.

In the next letter, dated five days later, February 5, 1943, both I and Aunt Selma express concern about not hearing from Mother, yet emphasizing our hope that she feels better. I further report that I like school and the advantage that it is so close to "home" . . . and proudly state that I can therefore walk to school by myself. "I am very, very, very well and happy. Aunt Selma has bought an entire set of new shoes for me, which gives me great pleasure." This time I close with five million kisses. (Inflation?)

It seems that telephoning was not included in the accepted procedures of the outside world contacting encamped refugees, nor vice versa. Therefore, as stated above, Aunt Selma expresses sustained anxiety about not hearing from mother, while expressing her repeated concern about mother's health. Later correspondence shows that mother did not get this letter in a timely fashion. Unbeknownst to us in St. Gallen, her health was, in fact, not improving. However, at the time of the writing, the Neuburgers already suspected that her cold may develop into bronchitis. This is precisely what happened, which brought on complications, namely kidney problems, which thank G-d were temporary and left no after-effects. Nevertheless, the Neuburgers again applied pressure on the authorities. Aunt Selma attached copies of their letters, which requested that mother and Neuburgers be informed about what is being done to restore mother to good health. The family is totally committed to finding a solution, she writes to mother. "Please let us know from your end whether or not you see any improvements. If not, my dear husband will have to intensify his efforts with the authorities. Please know that we are totally prepared and committed to have you released from camp and live with us . . . and that we are entirely at your disposal." (Note: Wow . . . truly exemplary!)

Aunt Selma then turns to the more mundane, confirming that indeed "Ernst seems to like school," and that I do my homework immediately upon coming home, meaning that the "fun and games" has to wait.

It seems that I continued to tell the story of our sad and dangerous experiences in Nazi-Germany and the conquered countries of Belgium and France, for Aunt Selma writes: "He exhibits unusual intuition and perception in the description of the event," and that the family finds it compelling and never tires listening to these stories in their full length.

In closing, Aunt Selma then inquires as to what mother is allowed to eat, so that "they" (again we/*wir*) can send her an appropriate package of goodies.

My next letter to Mother is dated February 11, 1943, informing her that I am *very* well and further advising her that I am sending to her "chocolates and bonbons" that I received as gifts. (Bingo! . . . spoiled already.) I continue by telling Mother that I like school more and more as the days go by, and that I made a friend. I write that I am waiting for mail from her, using the French word *poste*. Again, I send her regards from "Miss Hedi", who is obviously becoming an important friend. I send regards to some of the boys and girls I left behind at camp, adding "if they are still there." Again, five million kisses.

In her part of the letter, Aunt Selma is concerned about not getting an answer to her last letter. "Also", she continues, "we hope that we will soon receive a favorable reply from the authorities." She expresses hope that mother has recovered from her bronchitis attack. She reports that "Ernst is well and feels very much at home here." She adds that I have the daily company of a French immigrant playmate, who lives with friends of the Neuburgers. She thinks it's a plus to keep up my French.

[Author's note: I have absolutely no recollection of this child, nor has my mother. I don't even know if it was a boy or a girl. I can only assume that it was a very temporary situation. It makes the survival of this correspondence evermore valuable, for memory becomes faded and hazy. It is extremely unfortunate that I do not have Mother's letters in reply to "ours".]

In the meantime, I did acquire a weekend girl friend. She was six years old. Her name was Marion Kleinberger. Her mother died when she was two. She was being raised by her maternal grandparents in her father's house. The grandparents were the Neuburger's best friends and bridge buddies. So, when they got together on weekends for their frequent and regular game, both of us had a built-in playmate. Marion and I maintain contact to this very day. Marion wrote a very sweet letter to my mother on the occasion of a recent special birthday.

Back to the letter: Aunt Selma mentions that she had a letter from Aunt Martha, my grandmother's Swiss sister, who was—you will remember—mother's conduit to the Neuburgers. She adds that many of Aunt Martha's concerns are now obsolete due to Uncle David's letter to the camp commander.

Indeed it was at this time—and due to the Neuburgers' intensified efforts—that mother was transferred to a "better" camp, closer to St. Gallen, namely Camp Adliswil near Lake Zurich about fifty miles away. Camp Adliswil was a converted school building. It was more comfortable than Bueren. Mother also obtained leave to visit me in St. Gallen. However, due to her now almost chronic cold and bronchitis, she was not permitted to travel. Meanwhile, the Neuburgers were still waiting for mother's total release from the Swiss "camp system". It was never to be.

The next letter from St. Gallen in my possession is dated February 19, 1943. I had now been with the Neuburgers for one month.

Aunt Selma—with mention of, and regards from Uncle David—covers the following matters. As before—and in an equally kind tone—she reports that "Ernst is well and continues to enjoy school. Leisure time with him passes only too quickly." She adds that Anneliese*, the daughter of the above-mentioned Aunt Martha, and therefore a true first cousin of my father, is coming to visit on the weekend to finally meet "our young man". Aunt Selma places some cash in the envelope—spending money for my mother—a habit that became frequent and regular. Aunt Selma adds that the whole family is looking forward to finally meeting mother.

In my part of the letter, besides "the usual", I inform Mother that I had written post cards to the two teachers at Camp Bueren and to the Sachs family, new friends, also at Bueren. The number of kisses escalates to ten million. Miss Hedi adds her own note to the letter, saying that she hopes mother can get leave without further delay.

(*) Author's note: I pause to say a few words about Cousin Anneliese. She is two years older than Hanns, and they are the best of friends. She is the kind of person that upon meeting you feel that you have known her all of your life: open, warm and sunny, with a great sense of humor . . . pleasant to be with. She would play an important role during Mother's and my stay in Switzerland, as we will see. Anneliese lifted herself up by the bootstraps, out of the small Swiss village of her birth, out of genteel poverty, and into an important job. She would marry relatively late in life, to a wonderful man considerably her junior. He was a kind and attentive man, with a wonderful sense of humor as well. My wife and I had the pleasure of meeting him on one of our trips to Switzerland. They had a boy, named Ronnie, who would become very successful, and solidified the family's new socio-economic position. Then, suddenly and sadly, Anneliese's husband passed away. Other family tragedy would follow. However, Anneliese would never lose her compass in life, her ability to excel, and her wonderful laugh and sense of humor. She will be ninety years old in 2010. I saw her—and Ronnie and his family—on my most recent trip to Switzerland in the spring of 2009. But, more about that later.

On February 26, 1943, it seems that a short post card from me to Mother had to suffice. "I slept well. How are you, dear Mother?" Only "regards" this time; no kisses. However, two days later this card is quickly followed by a letter—also from Aunt Selma—and the ten million kisses reappear. I once again confirm that I have grown very accustomed to my new home; that I listen to "Gramafon" records every day; and that I have very neat toys leftover from the Neuburger "boys", especially an electric train set, complete with a very realistic station with ticket windows and all, and a bridge, and a road with a traffic barrier. (Author's note: Of course, there was a separate play/ toy room and a separate billiard/ping—pong room upstairs, and lots more room "downstairs" for arts and crafts activities, playing board games with a friend, or just plain play. This was still a time, before TV and electronic games, in which children were free to "just play" and let their imaginations roam freely and broadly.)

In Aunt Selma's portion, she doesn't miss the repeated opportunity to report how well Ernst has "assimilated to his new home." It is now exactly one month and two days after my arrival. Of course, much of this is intended to make mother feel good about her decision. Inquiring once again about mother's health, she repeats her inquiries about mother's long-lasting cold and bronchitis, and the health of her kidneys. The leave and the visit to St. Gallen did not materialize. "However, the whole family is looking for good news from you, Mrs. Kate." The rest is small talk and includes the mention of an immigrant family from Mannheim, who left Germany earlier than we did, and now resides in St. Gallen. They came to the Neuburger house for a visit in order to meet and greet me, as well as the Neuburgers. They apparently were friends of my parents in Mannheim. I have no recollection whatsoever of this Becker family and my encounter with them. (Note: the Swiss government made a very explicit bureaucratic differentiation between "immigrants" who settled in Switzerland before the war and "refugees" who crossed the borders after the start of the war.)

Unfortunately, the regularity and the continuance of the correspondence ends here, the remaining letters long lost or simply discarded. However, a letter dated April 30th of the same year did surface. As before, it is from St. Gallen and to my Mother. I have now been with the Neuburgers for three and a half months. It illustrates that my handwriting and German spelling and grammar is much improved. It acknowledges the receipt of a letter from Mother. It tells her how much I enjoyed receiving it. Further, it states that in the meantime, I had visited Aunt Martha in Diessenhofen . . . and that I had a good time. Her granddaughter Ellen, somewhat older than I, made for a good playmate, so it seems. I continue to report that (1) all's well in school and (2) that the weather is finally getting milder, enabling me to help Miss Hedi with her gardening. Kisses were deflated to one million. Half of the page is covered with a rather well-drawn, colored picture of a house and its surroundings. It's a very generic house, and certainly not the Neuburger's beautiful house. However, a bright sun shines down on it. (Note: Much of my correspondence to come—and especially birthday cards—is illustrated, obviously a product of the excellent schooling in Switzerland at any grade level.)

Aunt Selma, in her usual portion of the letter, writes that Uncle David has not been feeling well. Nevertheless, Anneliese is expected once again for a weekend visit. The letters from Aunt Selma have become far less formal. They have evolved from "Dear Mrs. Feibelmann" to Dear Mrs. Kate" to "Dear Ms. Kate" to "Dear Kate", and signed "Your Aunt Selma" rather than "Selma Neuburger". She also makes reference to attaching some food rationing stamps for mother.

In the interim, on April 9th of that year, there is a copy of Ernst's first report card in his handwriting. He has joined the ranks of the "average students", although "effort" and "conduct" in all six subjects received an A. He adds, that Uncle David and Hanns each gave him a one-Swiss Franc reward.

The available correspondence then skips forward to a joint-letter on the occasion of Mother's birthday on September 13, 1943. Besides good wishes, Ernst writes that Uncle David continues to be unwell, and that for the first time in some weeks has joined the family lunch, the big meal of the day in Europe. This is wonderful news for Ernst, as apparently a thoroughly loving relationship has developed between Ernst and his kind grandfatherly foster parent. It's very obvious and jumps from the paper of the letter. Ernst also writes that "Aunt Selma has sent to you an umbrella for your birthday. I contributed three Francs from my savings to this cause." His handwriting, spelling and grammar show continued significant further improvement, and now fall into the typical Swiss third grader mold: neat, clear and precise. These are the watchwords (no pun intended) of Swiss culture, and probably—perhaps to a somewhat lesser degree—that of all German speaking people of Europe. The letter is again illustrated by cheerful, multi-colored designs. I guess someone liked art class.

In Aunt Selma's—by now carved in stone—portion, she happily confirms that Uncle David's health is indeed improving, and expresses the hope that this improvement will continue. She regretfully notes and confirms that mother is now having some difficulties with her eyes. No details are discussed.

However, there seems to be some degree of unpleasant seriousness. She kindly wishes mother a quick and complete recovery, and warmly adds best wishes for her birthday. She adds words of hope for a satisfactory outcome of the war in the not too distant future, so that mother can be reunited with her husband and close family. In the closing of the letter, a few more comments about the umbrella are overshadowed by a sincere attempt to cheer up my mother, whose morale is obviously waning.

*   *   *

The last letter found from this immediate period is dated March 12, 1944. It is only from Ernst for reasons to follow. Again, it is cheerfully illustrated. He writes that a letter, addressed to the Neuburgers, has been received from mother. He hasn't opened it because Aunt Selma and Uncle David are in Basel visiting a specialist/physician. Obviously, Uncle David's health has relapsed again, a condition that would heartbreakingly continue until the end of his life. Ernst's resultant dark mood (G-d, how he loved that man . . .!) is reflected in his report that after a very snowy winter, it still continues to just snow and snow, and that after the briefest of thaws, it snowed again overnight. Speaking of "sad", he proceeds to report that he had just seen the movie "Bambi", having been invited by a Mrs. Schiff, a friend of Aunt Selma. Miss Hedi adds her regards in her own handwriting.

In retrospect, may I add that Spring did finally arrive. The gloom would soon lift for everyone in view of the Allied invasion of France. Allied victory was now almost certain. However, would it come in time to save at least two million Jews? Is Kate's treasured husband—my beloved Father—still alive? Would he survive this final phase of the war?

*   *   *

Also surviving is the text of a poem, written by Ernst—with someone's generous help (I seem to remember that it was Aunt Martha.)—to be recited on the occasion of a large party in honor of Uncle David's and Aunt Selma's twenty-fifth wedding anniversary, a few weeks after the war ended in 1945. At the war's end, Mother had finally joined the Neuburger household on a quasi-permanent basis. Ernst had passed his tenth birthday in late December 1944.

Back to Ernst's poem: After the usual congratulations, the poem thanks the celebrants for recognizing him as a true relative; for welcoming him so warmly into their beautiful home; for permitting him to stay for a long time; for spoiling him, and for being so very good to him. He continues—all in rhyme—that he cannot reciprocate; that G-d will furnish His reward to the Neuburger foster parents. Nonetheless—just in case, perhaps—Ernst repeats his thousand-fold thanks for all the good times. In the poem, he joyfully acknowledges his mother's presence, finally freed from the camp just days ago. He again thanks the Neuburgers for their willingness to help both him and his mother. He promises that after the imminent move to yet another foreign country, he will continue to show his appreciation for all their help and love. He ends with repeated good wishes and much luck for the anniversary couple and the entire "House of Neuburger".

With the greatest of sadness, I must report here that Uncle David passed away a few weeks later, his heart unable to carry on. He died on my mother's watch, in her arms. He had guided the family safely through the war. His task was completed. The enormous Nazi butchery and the immense danger to all of Europe had finally passed . . . and now, he must have reasoned, he could pass as well.

CHAPTER 11

Camp Montana

Beauty and Longing in the Alps

We pick up the narrative once again in March of 1943. In late February, Kate was finally transferred from the Swiss refugee camp at Bueren, to a camp in Adliswil, near Zurich. Ernst is with his foster family in St. Gallen.

The number of refugees continued to amass, and eventually expanded to one million. For a nation of only four million inhabitants the absorption of this tsunami of refugees became a major problem. Switzerland deserves only praise and admiration for the manner in which it managed this project. Every one of these desperate, down-beaten, exhausted, violently displaced persons was given a roof over their head, ample and nutritious food (army rations, in fact), health care, and in order to reduce boredom and stress (. . . and cost) the opportunity to work in the camp: the office, mail room, child care, laundry, cleaning detail—each according to his/her ability, education, experience and disposition.

It was at this time that the Swiss government made a momentous decision. The war had stopped all foreign tourism. Huge hotels, many in some of the well-known resorts stood empty and deserted. With a critical need for space, these hotels would make excellent minimum security camps. The transfer began almost immediately. In April 1943, my mother—due to her poor health and the nature of her illness—was moved to her third camp, a former grand hotel in Montana, a summer and winter resort of breathtaking beauty. It was, however, and certainly even by Swiss standards, very, very distant from St. Gallen. Later, my mother confided in me as to just how much she missed "her little boy." It was mutual. On the plus side, mother recovered quickly in Montana.

Now that the refugees were finally being settled in quarters and circumstances that would most likely prevail until the end of the war, a time period no one could predict, the Swiss government adopted a method calling for a very light hand in the administration of the camps. Where would the detainees go? Switzerland was totally surrounded by Nazi nations (Germany, Austria, Italy) and Nazi-occupied France. The camps were therefore run by just an Administrator and a Deputy Administrator. A larger staff was rare. The large majority of these administrators were women. With more than a tinge of anti-Semitism in high places, the Head Camp Administrator was usually chosen accordingly. It seems that there was no such litmus test for the deputies. At the Montana camp, a Frau Stricker, the Chief Administrator, fit the mold perfectly. She had two married sisters residing in Germany, both married to high-ranking SS officers. The deputy was a sweet, caring young woman named Gachnang with whom mother would develop a friendship that would last long beyond the war years.

One rule was strictly enforced—and mother believed rightly so—and that was the work rule. It was the only way to keep the daily life of the camp on an even keel. There would be no "outsourcing" for washing the laundry, cleaning the common areas of the vast camp building, nor the food service, nor maid service (joke). Individuals and their roommate(s) would be responsible for keeping their own rooms clean. Everyone was assigned to a work detail covering the various areas mentioned above. My mother worked in the office. She was an excellent worker and believed in doing the job right. A generous woman of character and humanity, she quickly formed genuine friendships, such as her roommate, a Margot Schott from Paris. Her husband was also in Montana. However, as previously mentioned, the current camp policy was to separate men and women. Also, there was a Dr. Lehman (a woman from Mannheim, mother's hometown), and—of course—mother's new and soon to be nearest friends, the Hermanns, whose names I would hear for many years to come. After the war, at mother's behest, the Hermanns, a lovely, intelligent, cultured, childless couple from Vienna, applied for—and received—permission to remain in Switzerland and settle in St. Gallen. The Neubuger family had pre-arranged excellent jobs for them, and they settled into a lovely apartment . . . and into a comfortable "second life". Mother and I would see them on our return travels as long as they both lived. Their English setters were as elegant as their masters.

Life at the Montana Camp was relatively pleasant, mother stated in her earliest reports. There was a curfew on weekdays. However, from Saturday noon until Sunday evening, the detainees could leave the camp at their leisure. Leave involving travel had to be approved by the authorities and required a travel permit. Yes, mother thought, here one could wait out the war's end, assuming Hitler did not invade Switzerland. In retrospect that was most unlikely. Certainly no experienced general would attack. However, Hitler's mercurial temperament was unpredictable. He was driven by bestial hate and an inferiority complex about the size of Texas. Would he go after those Jews in Switzerland? They were a part of his annihilation plans . . . and the museum for an extinct race. Well, as we all know now, he did not invade. Militarily, there was no advantage. The Nazis were permitted to run trains through Switzerland and through the tunnels of the mountain passes to Italy . . . no questions asked: Jews and political prisoners northbound, Nazi military personnel and materiel southbound. These railroad tunnels and roads would have been blown up and destroyed the second the first German soldier crossed the Swiss border. Mountain country is hard to take and easy to defend. Just one Swiss soldier could lob grenades down the mountain and/or hill all day long . . . or until he was taken out by one of the enemy's "big guns." The Germans would have taken substantial losses. Furthermore, panzers are not the best attack weapon in mountainous terrain. But more importantly, the Nazis appreciated Switzerland's neutrality. They considered it of substantial value in the exchange of spies, intelligence, and important prisoners. Most of all, the Swiss banks acted as a safe, secret depository for the Nazis' ill-begotten treasures, especially the gold. Ah yes, the gold . . . stolen from the Jews and from all enemies of the Third Reich: jewelry, coins, tooth fillings . . . "mountains" of it, melted down into ingots and placed into the bowels of Swiss banks. These were not just the property of the Reich, but also the property of the highest ranking Nazis in government and in the Armed Forces. Goering, Hitler's second in command, that fat air-force-blue—uniformed pig was a "great" art connoisseur . . . or perhaps just a connoisseur of stolen riches. Evil men and women who in 1945 would avoid the allied dragnet for war criminals, clandestinely picked up their loot in Switzerland and successfully escaped to Argentina and other fascist countries . . . and lived out their lives in relative luxury and peace. There is always the exception to prove the rule: Eichman, for example, as well as the few who ran into the extra-curricular activities of the Jewish Brigade, attached to the British forces in northern Italy in late 1944 and 1945 . . . and later the long arm of the global Israeli intelligence establishment.

The beauty, the peaceful and serene calm of Montana belied all these dangers, fears and speculations. Here my dear mother would make her stand, praying for peace, determined to "fight" once again if necessary.

And now, finally, Mother was permitted to visit St. Gallen for the first time. What a joyous reunion it was. You cannot possibly imagine mother's—and my—unbridled feelings of love . . . and the tears of joy that flowed that late-winter afternoon. Mother was astounded at the surroundings and the setting that was the Neuburger's beautiful, comfortable, warm and welcoming home. They embraced mother in the same fashion they had embraced me . . . unconditionally. Yet, everything hung once again on the importance of first impressions. Mother passed muster immediately, especially with Uncle David, that master of human personality, needs, and unspoken vibes. The entire family was there to greet mother. Walter, like his father, found these interpersonal moments easier than most. His heart could readily deal with the human condition. Of course that by no means intends to imply that Aunt Selma and Hanns were not at their most cordial and sincere at finally welcoming their house guest . . . the heroine of little Ernstli's life. Aunt Selma escorted mother to the guest room on the third floor, where she could for the first time in a long time enjoy the gift of privacy and total quiet. Communal life can get you down, mother once said. However, here she could—again for the first time in what seemed like eons—luxuriate in the memories of her parental home and her home with my father (and me). Tonight she would feel safe amid the turmoil that was Europe.

The dinner hour glowed in the warmth of this reception. Her stories intrigued the Neuburger family as had mine. My joy and pride brought on by my most wonderful mother must have been obvious to everyone at that bountiful table. The Neuburger's conclusion? My G-d, what this woman had to accomplish to save two lives. What rigors she had to survive to stay alive. Alone, the family destroyed, she battled on. The Neuburgers didn't miss a beat. They realized that they had just met a great lady. Mother was invited back again and again during the war and after our immigration to America. Their admiration for her had a lifespan of its own and continues this very day (2010). Hanns would call Kate regularly. I still speak to Hanns every Sunday. He never forgets to send regards to mother. At the wonderful age of 101, St. Gallen, Switzerland—mother recently told me—is one destination she would like to visit just one more time.

Sooner or later the evening had to end. Uncle David tired and I had school the following morning. However, that evening at "Number 40" has never been forgotten. What the whims of war and tragedy can forge! The entire weekend was simply marvelous. The Neuburger's generosity toward my mother, an almost total stranger, knew no limit. However, I already dreaded having to say goodbye once again . . . so did mother. However, neither of us could negate that moment of parting that would come only too soon. What good news then when I was told that plans had already been made for my visit to Camp Montana, a practice that the Swiss authorities greatly encouraged. It would be during the Easter vacation, another—even longer—solo train trip into uncharted waters. Nevertheless, my eager anticipation seemed to make the time pass quickly.

And so, the very first of my semi-annual visits to Montana was upon us. The reunion with my mother was different this time. It was not under the microscope of the Neuburgers. Yes, mother's new friends had assembled. But, that was somehow different. What it may have lacked in privacy, it made up in raw emotion. I immediately liked mother's Montana friends. They were lovely and immediately likeable. These visits would be a very helpful and soothing experience for both my mother and me. Naturally, proof once again that I had only one, irreplaceable mother and one unique mother-child relationship. Future visits were timed to coincide with the winter and summer school vacations. Mother's visits to St. Gallen would be about every six to eight weeks apart. Each and every reunion would be fireworks all over, at least for the moment . . .

Dinner that first night at Camp Montana was swell. That huge dining hall, the buzz, the energy made a whole new impression on me. It was good to be here. I would sleep on a folding bed erected in my mother's room, along with her and her roommate, the lovely Madame Schott, who we would later, in 1946, visit in Paris before leaving the European continent. Great! . . . and I mean that in a most positive sense. I knew that I would sleep well after that long, tiring trip, and the added bonus of sleeping under a mother's watch—and affection—once again. Yet, something inside me couldn't wait to get into that winter wonderland and the breathtaking landscape that was Crans-Montana.

Montana, and its twin resort village Crans, is situated in a mountain resort area of immense beauty in the Canton of Valais, the French-speaking part of the Alpine massif, high above the Rhone River, which eventually flows into Lake Geneva and on into France. Crans-Montana's mountain is the south side of the Wildstrubel, a 10,000 "footer". On a Swiss map, one can best locate Crans-Montana as being across the Rhone valley, opposite the famous Matterhorn. Need I say more? At this time of the year, the entire area was still a snow-covered wonderland. In summer it could claim the highest-in-elevation golf course in Europe at that time. The still-wintry temperature was crisp, but the April sun was gaining strength every day. The holiday skiers of all ages—some dressed in shorts and only light tops—were everywhere. I was overwhelmed by such natural beauty. The Neuburgers had made sure that I would be properly dressed for this winter paradise, proper boots and all. One could safely walk everywhere . . . and my mother and I did, of course nearly always with the usual entourage of her three (sometimes four) best friends.

Albeit through the eyes of an eight-year-old, I soon observed that the camp was well-run by the two Swiss administrators and especially by the internees, who cooperated in a self-forged system of making the camp internally secure, clean, healthy and comfortable, while dispensing good food. The internees, on their Army rations, seemed well-fed and content in what certainly seemed to be a fair and equitable arrangement all around. The children seemed well cared-for and in good health and spirits. They had built-in playmates from the first day they arrived there. They shared a common experience and a common fate. They were with their parents . . . or at least with their mothers. They attended the village school, which was excellent . . . like all Swiss schools. To the best of my knowledge, this latter arrangement proceeded without serious incident, even resulting in friendships with "the locals". This isn't bad, I said to myself in a first flicker of renewed doubt about my parental separation: "Why? . . . why me?"

CHAPTER 12

The Family

Victims and Survivors

I
Grandmother Strauss

As satisfactory as conditions in Montana and in St. Gallen may have appeared on the surface, the gnawing, stress—and anxiety—producing 24/7 worry on Kate's mind was not only her husband's fate, but also that of her closest and dearest relatives. Her mother, Frieda Strauss (nee Haas), a widow, to whom my mother was extremely close, accompanied by a Strauss sister-in-law, Regina Strauss, was deported—in the Fall of 1940—from Mannheim to Gurs, a lethal concentration camp near the Vichy-France town of Oloron, near Lourdes, in the Basses-Pyrenees region, close to the Pyrenees Mountains and the Spanish border. My maternal grandmother, Frieda, had been stricken with a stroke on Kristallnacht in 1938 and was to remain a bedridden, wheel chair-bound invalid all her life. In late 1941, due to her condition, she—along with her sister-in-law—was mercifully transferred to Recebedou (sic). The French authorities reluctantly permitted the local nuns to visit the camp once a week. With the greatest of kindliness and humanity, the nuns ministered whatever physical and spiritual aid they could possibly give. Their attention was soon drawn to my grandmother and her worthy companion, without whom she never would have survived. The nuns decided to make these two ladies a special focus of their weekly visits. As the conditions in the camp—and the treatment of the internees worsened the holy sisters of the local convent, without saying a word (for their own security reasons) decided to rescue these two poor souls. On the next visit they brought along two vestments. They waited for the appropriate moment and quickly changed the two Jewish ladies into them. And so, my grandmother was wheeled out of the camp by one of the nuns, while her companion, Aunt Regina Strauss, walked—as best she could—arm-in-arm with the other nuns . . . out of the camp . . . and as quickly as possible to the Convent of St. Rambert-sur-Loire. At bed-check they were missed of course and immediately listed as escapees. The following morning, members of the vile, despicable, collaborative French camp security forces headed straight for the convent. They truly believed that their uniforms, by this time tailored to clone the German model as closely as possible for maximum terror effect, would surely intimidate the brave, sensitive and patriotic Mother Superior. They forcefully knocked on the large solid wood door. Indeed, Mother Superior opened the door. The head camp guard told the "head nun" that he had every reason to suspect that she was harboring two Jewish escapees, which she politely denied. He then demanded to enter and be permitted to search the premises. Taking a determined step toward him, as if to stiffen her resistance, she informed him that no man is permitted into the convent and its grounds, which he as a good French Catholic would surely be aware of. He relented and left, only to return regularly, always to encounter the same script. Mercifully, this was not the SS making the inquiries. They were engaged elsewhere, especially as the Nazi juggernaut began to falter and grind to a halt in Russia and in North Africa. Miraculously, and with the greatest of gratitude to the Covent and its order, my grandmother and her sister-in-law, herself a saint among women, survived. At the end of the war, the Sisters successfully contacted the Jewish-French Federation and its newly formed section for the search and care of refugees. The two ladies were transported to St. Antoine, a suburb of Nice, where the Federation had always administered a Jewish old-age home.

Among the beauty that is the mountainous landscape above Nice and the azure waters of the Mediterranean, the two ladies lived out their lives. In March 1946, Alfred, my mother's much younger brother, would be the first in the family to visit his mother and Aunt Regina. Mother and I visited them before leaving the European continent in 1946. The joy of this reunion can hardly be fully recorded here. It was an outpouring of the love and eternal bond between a daughter and her mother, plus a beloved aunt and caretaker . . . all strong, brave women. It was a moment of loveliness that only peace could bring. It was a victory lap for the four survivors . . . and perhaps several more in the extended family. There was, of course, the dark overlay of my father's cruel death at Auschwitz. My grandmother loved my father like a son.

We spent lovely, leisurely days with the two ladies. There were volumes to discuss, especially since my mother's much younger brother—and only sibling—also survived the Holocaust, albeit under horrifying circumstances we will discuss later in this chapter. He would visit the ladies again during the following year. When time to part finally came, we optimistically did not say goodbye; we said au revoir. And fortunately, I was able to visit my dear grandmother again in 1950 on my first trip back to Switzerland, where I spent my entire summer vacation with the Neuburger family. In 1952, on my mother's first return trip to Europe to attend Hanns Neuburger's wedding, mother visited Nice again. As reported in beautiful letters, the two ladies and my mother had such a grand time. It would be the last time Kate would see her mother and her aunt, the two brave ladies, who stared down death and disaster, and somehow managed to cope and to survive and to literally squeeze a few more good years out life. I was the last to see them one more time in 1953, when I returned once again to spend the summer in Switzerland. I had a few wonderful days with these two dearest of ladies. They had maintained their sense of humor. They were health-wise quite unchanged since 1946, and they were extremely well cared for by "the home". In those years that no one from the immediate family was able to visit, Selma Neuburger—and her son Hanns—traveled to the Riviera to see "the ladies". It turned out that they also—year after year—showed their gratitude, in large part on my mother's behalf, to the lovely, kind, young couple, the Schoenfelds, that administered the home, in terms of totally voluntary monetary gifts, plus the latest fashions from their ladies' apparel manufacturing plant for Mrs. Schoenfeld, who was a nurse by profession. Out of pure new friendship, gratitude and mutual respect, favors of a different kind lasted for a long time after the ladies were deceased. The Neuburgers eventually brokered a job for the Schoenfelds in Switzerland. They were engaged as the administrators of a year-round health facility for Jewish children who—according to the state of the art of the medical profession circa 1954 or 1955—benefited from living at the elevation of the foothills of the Swiss Alps. Such was—to emphasize it once again—our relationship with the Neuburger family . . . and such was their love and generosity for our entire family.

In May 1954, at age eighty, our wonderful and blessed Aunt Regina passed away. My grandmother, now seventy-three years old, frail and grieving her cherished companion's loss, died four months thereafter. They were sorely missed by the entire family and all who knew and loved them, including my grandmother's surviving brothers who lived in America, but never had the opportunity to see them after the war.

II
The Feibelmann Grandparents.

My paternal grandparents, Sigmund and Frieda Feibelmann lived in Ruelzheim, a small German town with a relatively large Jewish population. My grandfather, a son of Jakob Feibelmann, was born in 1865. My grandmother (nee Rosenthal . . . and yes, another Frieda) was born in 1873. The morning after *Kristallnacht*, they moved to Mannheim. At first they lived with us, but shortly thereafter were able to rent rooms with a Jewish family. They were also deported to Gurs in 1940. My father was also, in time, sent to Gurs, and was able to lend some assistance to his parents, his mother-in-law and the other relatives. However, only too soon my father was transferred. Shortly thereafter, my grandparents were separated. My dear paternal grandmother, Frieda, at the age of seventy-two, was transferred to a camp near Macon, where—unbeknownst to my mother—she passed away just one month after Germany's surrender. Once my father had arrived at the camp at Des Milles my grandfather requested, and, surprisingly received, a transfer to Des Milles. At least father and son were reunited. Des Milles was close enough to Marseilles so that my mother and I could visit and bring food packages (halva was a special favorite) and some adequate clothing. On November 23, 1943, shortly after my father's deportation, my grandfather died at the age of seventy-eight. In his prime a stately, tall, strong man, he always loved my mother very much. He—along with all the family members mentioned in this chapter so far—were all wonderful human beings, whose lives were ruined and shortened at the pleasure of Herr Hitler.

III
Brother Alfred

Kate's brother and only sibling was thirteen years younger than her. Born of the same parents in 1921, he was eleven years old when Hitler and his henchmen took over. As alluded to in an earlier chapter, it was this age group who suffered most in the earliest years of the Nazi regime. They had maximum exposure in the schools and on the streets. When it became too dangerous for these boys and girls to attend the German public schools, Alfred was sent to a private engineering school in Berlin. Thanks to my mother's perseverance, Alfred was on "the list" for the Kindertransport, a last minute international effort to save the children. He had the extraordinary luck to be on the last transport out of Germany. The Germans held up the train at the Dutch border. The Dutch government quickly and urgently brokered its passage stating humanitarian reasons. The transport proceeded to its original destination, namely Great Britain. The very young children were taken in by British families, preferably in the towns and cities beyond London. The older children—particularly the boys—were sent to a vocational school in Leeds, run by O.R.T., the world-wide charitable Jewish educational organization.

Alfred Strauss was just shy of eighteen years of age when he arrived at Leeds. Great Britain entered the war and quickly suffered near fatal defeat at Dunkirk. The British government, still under Prime Minister Chamberlain, panicked and feared an imminent German invasion of the British Isles. As a result of this, these young Jewish males were considered a security risk, and in part interned. Unfortunately, the British government, with more than a hint of anti-Semitism, did not see these newly arrived Jewish youngsters as having been given political asylum from the Nazi regime, but rather categorized them as German Enemy Aliens. These boys were immediately shipped to British internment camps. However, this move was still not deemed "secure" enough. Within a short time these youths, combined with new, German military prisoners of war resultant from the action at the coastline of northwestern France, were loaded on two British personnel-carrying ships. Destination: Australia. The journey immediately turned into a living hell for these Jewish boys, a small contingent of eighteen youngsters. The British naval crew robbed, beat and tortured them. For example, bored—and often drunk—the Brits broke beer bottles on the deck and forced the boys to run over them. At this early stage of the war, German u-boats had full control of the seas in the North Atlantic and the west coast of Africa. Correctly identifying the two ships as British transports, they could not know that they carried German prisoners of war. They promptly attacked the ships with torpedoes, sinking the first ship and slightly damaging the second, before realizing that most of the bodies floating in the water had German uniforms and insignias. They stopped the attack at once, and ship No. 2 sailed on with its eighteen Jewish boys.

The attacks on the Jewish boys did not stop however. The German prisoners—ordinary members of the Wehrmacht—also young and inexperienced, worried about their own bleak prospects and immediate future, sailing farther and farther away from their homeland and families with every passing minute—and separated from their officers—made every attempt to protect the Jews. (Yes, you read correctly!) They were rebuffed by their British, obviously unsupervised captors. When the Germans' efforts remained to be hopelessly unsuccessful, they designated a committee and an impromptu leader to address the ship's captain. The former told the captain that although his men were unarmed, they so overwhelmingly outnumbered the Brits on board that a mutiny could not be ruled out. The captain got the message loud and clear. He agreed that these attacks must be halted and issued orders immediately. The attacks on the Jews stopped. The Brits became rather wary of their prisoners. The Germans continued to befriend and protect the boys in every way, and the Jews gratefully accepted and encouraged this friendship.

The entire assorted "passenger" contingent disembarked in Sydney, and was sent to a desert tent camp two-hundred miles from Sydney. Their Australian "hosts" were far kinder. Weeks had passed and the Australian press began to report stories about Nazi war crimes and anti-Semitic horrors in Austria and Poland. Everyone connected with the camp read or heard these news reports. When the Red Cross packages began to arrive, the Australians made sure the Jewish boys got theirs first; only then came the Germans' turn. When the Germans readily accepted this procedure, the Aussies began to learn more and more about the bond that had formed aboard ship. However, life in the Australian bush was hard on all the Europeans. It was beastly hot and there were few comforts. There were, however, the scorpions and the "bugs". Alfred contracted rheumatic fever and was transferred to a Sydney hospital. This in fact broke the story of the eighteen (now seventeen) Jewish boys in the desert. A Sydney Rabbi immediately "ran" with the story. The entire Australian Jewish community was up in arms. The Rabbi traveled to the camp at once, simultaneously receiving government permission to bring the boys to Sydney. So enraged was the Australian population and the press that Winston Churchill, now finally installed as Prime Minister, heard about the story, and insisted that the boys be shipped back to England immediately. He was warned of the dangers of yet another ocean voyage in u-boat infested waters. Rather typically, he would not relent. The only way to right this wrong, he insisted, was to repatriate these young victims of Nazi hate and British bigotry to English soil, and see to their care and education. He instructed the navy to draw up the safest possible sea route, which included several stops at west-African ports. Alfred had recovered sufficiently to join his seventeen brethren on the long but successful voyage.

[Note: This incident, affecting eighteen young, scared, insecure Jews was not England's only transgression in such matters. Later, in December 1941 for example, the ship "Struma" left Romania bound for Palestine carrying 769 Jews. But, it was later denied permission by the British authorities to disembark. After a three-months delay, it was forced to return. Sailing through the Black Sea, it was intercepted by a Soviet submarine and sunk as an "enemy target."]

Back on English soil, Alfred was returned to the O.R.T. school. Because of his technical background at the Berlin school, he was assigned to learn tool making. During a routine inspection of the O.R.T. school, he was deemed old enough to enter into a job in industry. Universal, war-time call-up to military service had created a shortage of available labor. New hands were eagerly put to work at once. To facilitate his work arrangement, he was able to maintain his accommodations and meals at the O.R.T. school.

In January 1943, the Allies began to plan for the invasion in France. The American Army was looking for German-speaking personnel to be used in intelligence and counter-intelligence work, to be deployed immediately after the anticipated future collapse of Nazi-Germany. Alfred was thus recruited, having done some similar work for MI5. Training began at once, and in 1945, at the appointed time, Alfred was sent to Bremerhafen as a civilian attached to the U.S. Seventh Army. He wore an American military uniform with a small arm patch indicating civilian status. The Germans, however, had no idea. Later, he often told me about his remarkable experience with the American military forces. He often spoke of the warmth and welcome his American superiors and colleagues extended to him. I knew I was "home", he once said to me. In March 1946, he received compassionate leave to travel to Nice. He was overjoyed to see his mother and Aunt Regina. He had not seen them for seven years. He also went to visit the nuns of St. Rambert-sur-Loire. Later, he would often speak of this truly outstanding group of dedicated women. He would repeat his trip to Nice in 1947 before leaving Europe and the American military, at which time he emigrated to America to join the rest of the family. He loved America. He became a great friend and confidant.

IV
The Lowenbergs

My father's sister and only sibling, Dora (later changed to Dorothy) married Sally (later changed to Sol) Lowenberg in January 1923. They had one child, a son named Fritz (later changed to Fred). With the aid and assistance of relatives residing in Birmingham, England, they too fled Germany at the eleventh hour. In London, Sally and Dora were forced to find jobs as quickly as possible. Fred, age fifteen at the time, was soon interned and sent to the Isle of Man for the same reason reported above. He was finally released and found work. The Lowenbergs rented an apartment in a small row-house. Their cousins, two young women whose parents were deported by the Nazis, rented the other apartment. Sally Lowenberg was an affluent shoe retailer in the wine country region of Germany, namely in a town named Nassau. He was able to—and did—spoil his attractive, significantly younger wife. They traveled and lead the good life. However, in London they found a harsh and difficult life. Work was far too physically demanding for the aging Sally. Dora went to work as a seamstress. The German bombardment, the dreaded Blitz, started and went on for two years. This added great stress and danger to everyday life. I won't go into this perilous period in detail because everything you heard, everything you read, everything Edward R. Murrow reported was true. The Lowenbergs, along with millions of London residents, slept in subway stations. Every individual's allotted space was approximately the length and width of his or her body. Entire families, some with small children, took shelter underground. At sunrise, they left the subway and rushed to their little apartment. They paused as they rounded the corner of their street and checked to see if the house was still standing. They quickly washed, had breakfast and then went back to the subway station for the commute to work. Daytime bombing was routine and frequent. Employers took whatever precautions were possible and practical, conforming to government regulations and directives. At the end of the workday, a similar routine was repeated. Take the subway home. Then, quickly and foremost, shop for dinner. Food products were rationed and in short supply. After all, at this time in history Great Britain was losing the war. Not only had continental Europe become Greater Nazi-Germany, but the British were also losing their colonies one by one, mainly to the Japanese. After seeing, once again, that their home had survived the daytime bombings, they would quickly prepare dinner and eat. Then they would grab their "stuff" and be off to the subway station, cum public shelter and sleeping area. This would "get old" very fast. This routine was extremely stressful on the Lowenbergs and their newly-met English country men and women. Fortunately, the Brits were an extremely disciplined, orderly, and law-abiding people. They carried on under the guidance of their wartime hero, Winston Churchill. As a people and as a nation, they coped and they survived. In 1947, the Lowenbergs also joined the family in New York.

V
The Haas Family.

My mother's mother, Frieda Straus, nee Haas, had eight siblings, four brothers and four sisters. Two brothers immigrated to America as young, single men in the 1920's. The rest of "the clan" remained in Germany. The two remaining brothers, Ferdinand and Isidor, were to become partners in a wholesale distributorship of food and grain in Wiesbaden, Germany. They built their business into a large company by means of their hard work, smarts and modern business methods. In other words, they were way ahead of the curve.

They became wealthy, which only entrenched their position of family co-patriarchs. In an already close-knit family, they were especially close, beloved and respected. Ferdinand and his wife, Alice, had one child, a daughter, Lore, born in 1922. (As of this writing she is still alive and reasonably well. She is fourteen years younger than my mother. She's a dear, lovely soul, very close to my mother and the rest of the family.) Isidor lost his wife prematurely. Having no children, he moved in with his brother and family at the big house in Wiesbaden, an arrangement that happily lasted until the war and the Holocaust separated them.

In the early 1930's their business—rather counter-intuitively—continued to prosper and grow. When Hitler took power in January 1933, the Haas brothers were not overly concerned. Growing up in perhaps modern Germany's most liberal years, between the end of the Franco-Prussian War and World War One, they truly believed that Hitler would be gone shortly . . . unacceptable to the German people and the German body politic.

They were not alone in this assumption. However, Hitler, with the aid and support of the industrialists and the old aristocracy, quickly reopened the factories, put people back to work, and began huge infrastructure building programs. Germany already had social programs (e.g., social security for the elderly, etc.) since the time of Bismark. The economy flourished and the people were content for the first time since WWI. Result: Hitler was not going away soon.

Germany's Jewish population, relatively small and never over one percent, began to worry. But not all Jews! The Jewish population split into two groups: the pro-emigrationists and the anti-emigrationists. With the usual 20/20 hindsight, I can't begin to imagine how the latter got traction. Some of the Jewish organizations—associated with the "Federation"—were quite vocal in expressing their anti-emigration stance based on their reasoning that Jews had lived in Germany for at least a thousand years and had every right now to continue living there. They wrote letters to the Nazi government in Berlin stating their case. They never received a single reply. The Nazis had a good laugh and the letters ended up in "File 13". The Jewish organizations maintained their wrong-headed, now totally obsolete and perilous position far too long. Rabbis preached anti-emigrationism from the pulpit with equally naïve zeal. These two neo-assimilationist sources' opinions were gratefully and quickly adopted by anti-emigrationist individuals and families who wished to reinforce and justify their own potentially fatal position.

In our family, my father (!), the Haas brothers and the Feibelmann grandparents were among the anti-emigrationists. My mother, her brother, Alfred, and their mother, Frieda, were pro-emigrationists. Sadly, they were left to unsuccessfully chafe at their tether for the next several years. When my mother and father got married several months after Hitler's inauguration, the grandparents Strauss strongly suggested that instead of the customary grand tour of Italy, they travel to the U.S.A. They begged them to just look around and get the feel of the land. Many relatives had immigrated to America, some as far back as the 1860's. Many had prospered. The honeymooners would not be "alone". Yes, America was in the midst of the Great Depression. However, during the first couple of years of the Nazi regime, German-Jewish emigrants could have taken their money with them. The confiscatory policies (i.e. *Reichfluchtssteuer*) had not yet started. My father totally rejected the idea. "America?" he said; "America is for the Indians." The anti-emigrationists in the family were quick to support him. Kate & Company cringed. In early December 1934, grandfather Strauss died prematurely of natural causes. Notwithstanding the fact that many medical advancements were still very much in their infancy, it can nonetheless be said that the real cause of his death was medical malpractice. Later that same month, I was born. The birth of a son, in a country that soon was to disenfranchise him and every other Jew in Germany, should have been sufficient reason for my father and the other anti-emigrationists in the family to re-examine their flawed thinking. However, they did not. Business continued to flourish. Many Jews still felt safe and secure. As conditions for the Jews worsened, however, fewer and fewer held out. Finally in early 1937, my father consented to the request of an Affidavit from the wealthiest of our American relatives, the Erlanger family. Related on the Strauss side, they quickly obliged. When it arrived, my father changed his mind! The Affidavit was transferred to the Schloss family. (No relation to Brussels Schloss'.) Martha Schloss was a Haas cousin. She and her husband and their two sons left Germany as fast as possible, even though the confiscatory exit policies were now strictly enforced. In other words, like so many others before and after them, they left Germany penniless, the main thing being that they were out of Germany and out of danger. Good for them. They settled in New York. Mother and I have cordial contact with the two sons and their respective families to this very day.

The three Feibelmanns remained behind. In the understatement of the year, my mother was . . . "disappointed". Shortly thereafter, my father relented to at least request a new affidavit from the Erlangers. As late as the winter 1937-1938, my mother and I, and some of her friends, vacationed in the beautiful resort of Arosa, Switzerland. In her daily telephone calls to my father, mother begged him to simply pack a small suitcase and join us. He steadfastly refused. Mother and I returned to Germany.

The newest Affidavit once again arrived with great promptness. Several other American relatives joined in its sponsorship. Unfortunately, it was in fact too late. As the Depression in America failed to ease appreciably and fascist American groups—including German-American organizations—unleashed their anti-Semitic attacks, America's quota for the admission of European Jews became infinitesimal . . . an outrage for an alleged democracy and a serious blot on Roosevelt's legacy. Late in 1938 *Kistallnacht* followed . . . and you, dear reader, know the rest of that story.

The Haas brothers—and the entire senior contingent of the family—finally realized their lack of vision over these many years, their lack of knowledge of the world-at-large, and their fatalistic attachment to their assets, and to the German nation and its people. For all but Uncle Ferdinand, his wife and daughter, it was too late. In early 1942, Uncle Isidor, Ferdinand's brother and business partner, bought his way into *Theresienstadt,* the concentration camp established in November 1941 near Prague, Czechoslovakia. For a considerable time, the Nazis used it as a so-called model concentration camp vis-à-vis international inspection pressures and organizations such as the Red Cross. It was also served as a Nazi propaganda tool. At first Uncle Isidor may have considered himself one of the lucky ones. Although it is recorded that in October 1942 the first transport from Theresienstadt arrived at Auschwitz, Uncle Isidor was not amongst them, thereby at least avoiding that brand of horror. Nevertheless, he sadly perished at Theresienstadt.

Uncle Ferdinand and his family finally—and luckily—got out of Germany at the very last moment. With the help of Aunt Alice's brother and sister-in-law residing in Santo Domingo, the Haas trio obtained a very expensive visa from the Dominican Republic's embassy in Germany. They sailed to the Dominican Republic and stayed with their relatives for a few weeks, only to discover that a Dominican Republic visa obtained in that manner is good for any country on the planet, except the Dominican Republic. They were expelled as illegal aliens . . . luckily to the U.S.A., where they were held at Ellis Island as illegal aliens. Luckily as of this time and date, the U.S.A. no longer deported incoming Jews. However, they could not leave Ellis Island until one of them secured a job. Aunt Alice did just that, answering an ad placed by an affluent Jewish-American family residing in Brooklyn looking for housekeeper/cook. She, like so many German *Hausfrauen*, was an excellent cook. Her former station in life did not—due to her healthy and courageous mindset—preclude her entering into service, as the British would say. In return—and in addition to her small salary—she received a small room in which Uncle Ferdinand could live with her. The daughter, Lore, simultaneously found a sleep-in job as a nanny to the family of a Fifth Avenue urologist. Well played, I'd say.

However, America had still not entered the war. The Great Depression had still not ended. Jobs were hard to find, especially for a sixty-year-old former ueber-merchant from Germany, lacking all English language skills. Uncle Ferdinand was not to be discouraged. He soon noticed that an elderly Italian man came down his street—and through the surrounding neighborhood—every day with a horse-drawn wagon. The man was selling fresh produce. One could hear the bell on his cart and he would further announce his presence by calling out to the homeowners and their domestics. When the produce purveyor came around the next time, Uncle Ferdinand rushed down to the street. In the most broken English . . . and in hand signals—or whatever—he managed to communicate with the produce man. He told him, that he had noticed that he was very busy and obviously needed an assistant. The produce man replied that he did not need a helper at all. "Of course you do," replied Uncle Ferdinand. "Just think how much more territory you could cover, how much more merchandise you could sell, how much more money you could make." The produce man still shook his head with a definite no. "Look, I'll work for free for a couple of days. If you don't make more money you'll be rid of me," replied Uncle Ferdinand. I guess that was an offer the kindly old man could not refuse. The new venture was a complete and instant success. And that's how it came about that Uncle Ferdinand entered the produce business in a strange mega-metropolis in a strange country.

America entered the war very soon thereafter. Uncle Ferdinand found a job with a yarn company on Manhattan's Houston Street. Aunt Alice did likewise, leaving service with the Brooklyn family who were very kind and respectful. Uncle Ferdinand and Aunt Alice rented a small apartment near Broadway and 139th Street in Manhattan. Their best friends from Wiesbaden, also newly arrived in the U.S.A., lived in the same apartment house. They were happy for now and quickly adjusted to their newest lifestyle. (Much to be admired here!) As for any attraction to the old homeland, they would occasionally visit the Yorkville section of Manhattan. Its epicenter was at

Third Avenue and 86th Street. (Yes, The Elevated was still running.) It was the Gentile "Little Germany", *Bund* meetings and all. Not too many Germans lived there any longer. They had moved to Queens and the suburbs beyond. Nevertheless, for them, Yorkville's strong attraction remained. The German cafes and restaurants—such as the Café Geiger—remained open, busy, and a magnet for all Germans. The German butcher shop, complete with its large selection of *Wurst* remained operative, as did the German bakery, etc., etc. Uncle Ferdinand was much intrigued . . . and he was paying attention.

When the war ended in 1945, Uncle Ferdinand quickly surmised that these fine German-American citizens, never amused in the least that the American *Luftwaffe* had bombed the stuffing out of just about every city and town in Germany, thereby putting their dearest and closest relatives into harm's way. The American government and the military leadership wanted unconditional surrender . . . and that's what they got. It is not an overstatement to say that Germany was completely destroyed. Uncle Ferdinand correctly assumed that the weary, bombed-out, beaten-up surviving German population would literally need everything to survive the harsh winters of 1945/1946 and 1946/1947 and all the days in between. He further felt that their American relatives would not let them down in delivering all the aid and support they could muster. Time was of the essence. Ferdinand rented a tiny store in Yorkville, just off Third Avenue on 84th Street. Perfect! His knowledge of the food industry was, of course, most helpful. His English language skills were not much improved. However, this in no way impeded him to approach some of the biggest packaged food manufacturers directly, wheel and deal a little, and procure special prices in return for volume commitments. After all, everybody likes a bargain . . . and Uncle Ferdinand knew all about "loss leaders" and such. He hung out his "shingle". It simply read "Haas". (Exh.) The plan was to send food packages to the German WWII survivors.

He was questioned—and severely criticized—by relatives and friends . . . all survivors of the Nazi-regime and the concentration camps located in Germany (e.g. Dachau) about doing business with the "Germans". He replied that the German-American gentile's money was just as green as anyone else's, and that it was now emphatically his job and his duty to build a life for his family in his new adoptive homeland. He won that argument. Good for him once more. He was sixty-five years of age.

The people began to come . . . and they continued to come. "Haas" was a hit in Yorkville, especially on Saturdays, when tumult ruled at 225 East 84th Street. The tiny store was packed all day, for that matter almost every day, six days a week. His customers genuinely liked Ferdinand and Alice, his wife. In Uncle Ferdinand they recognized an expert in his field. He was imaginative and creative, thorough, prompt and honest. His customers trusted him. They felt safe and secure in the knowledge that he placed their satisfaction first. And, he spoke their language. Soon, the supply packages went beyond food items. A black market developed in Germany. The "trinity" of greatest trading value was cigarettes, coffee and flints. Yes, flints. The German surrender conditions prohibited the manufacture of ammunition. Matches fell under these rules . . . hence flints. There was a tremendous markup in this tiny item. You bought it in bulk and sold it by the dozen or the gross in little glassine envelopes. It was not all that long before the Allied Occupation Forces and the new Provisional Government stepped in to prevent the further and rapid growth of the black market. They prohibited the importation of cigarettes into Germany. Not to worry . . . Uncle Ferdinand found a small canning company in New Jersey, where the cigarettes were canned and labeled "tomato sauce". The American relatives would write to the German relatives, 'We hope you enjoyed the special tomato sauce with your pasta.' Bingo.

When business grew and grew, Uncle Ferdinand opened a second store at 1615 First Avenue. Aunt Alice's participation and assistance was invaluable from day one. When rapid delivery became a requirement, Uncle Ferdinand set up a Danish distributorship. The need and the shipments lasted well beyond the Spring of 1947; it unexpectedly ran into the 1950's and 1960's. In the early years the German population literally needed everything, from bicycle tires and tubes to blankets and other household ware. "Haas" shipped it all. Although, just about all the New York refugee relatives worked part-time in Uncle Ferdinand's "store" at one time or another, he hired a full time assistant, an efficient, friendly German-speaking Gentile lady. When Uncle Ferdinand reached his 80th birthday, he sold the business to her. After fifteen years, the business still had intrinsic value. Uncle Ferdinand did not retire. That was not his nature, nor his style. He worked in his nephew's retail stores on Manhattan's west side, not afraid to climb a ladder or carry a heavy package, if that was the need and the task. When he was ninety—and his wife eighty—his daughter, Lore, insisted that they move to Nashville, where she could keep an eye on them. Happy to be with their daughter and her family, they lived in a lovely apartment. But, Ferdinand, a dynamo all his life, was terribly bored by the life in the provincial southern city. He and his wife traveled back to New York at the slightest provocation and opportunity: Some distant cousin's special birthday or another's wedding or Bar-Mitzvah.

At the age of one hundred he welcomed the governor of Tennessee at the Y's swimming pool. He danced at his birthday party . . . and again later at his granddaughter's wedding. He was bright, alert and informed. He was great company. We had the pleasure of seeing him—and Aunt Alice—at both of these happy occasions. One sunny morning, at the age of one hundred one and a half, he gently collapsed into his egg . . . dead. Great way to go; great way to end a remarkable life . . . and a great story.

His miscalculations on the emigration issue were long forgotten and forgiven . . . and rightly so. These men—and women—were forced to deal with a hellish, enigmatic and insolvable problem. We, with advantage of hindsight and history, may not criticize them. Rather, we must recognize their struggle and their courage. The dignity of the Elders will never be threatened . . . at least not on my watch.

CHAPTER 13

"Papa"

"To be a German Jew in those years was impossible; to also be
a father and a husband required him to carry burdens, perhaps
unspoken, that we will never truly fathom. Confronted by such
responsibilities in such frightening and helpless times, he did
the very best he could. I will always see him as a heroic figure."
Quoted from a letter written by my good friend William J.
Crerend after reading the first draft of this paragraph in late
November 2009.

At this time—and before we return to the narrative—I would like to speak
about my late and beloved father, who suffered a doubly-ill fate. First came
the horror of Dachau. Then, almost four years later he was permanently
separated from his wife and child in a most twisted turn of tragic events, to
be transported to certain death in Auschwitz. Neither he nor the millions of
other innocent victims like him—men, women and children—deserved such
a calamitous fate. Yet, the question could very well be 'To what extent did he
contribute to his fate?' However, that question is not germane. Hindsight is
always biased. The volumes of history are filled with hindsight bias.

As reported in previous chapters, the majority of German—and Western
European Jewry in general—did not immediately panic upon Hitler's ascent
to power in January 1933. Yet, Adolph Hitler's "Mein Kampf", the book
that later had to be present in every German-gentile home, conspicuously
displayed, and at least theoretically read, should have been Reading
Assignment No.1 on that January day for every Jew in Germany and beyond.
Read it and believe it! How often does history follow a published game plan?

However, Hitler's implementation of the dreaded Jew-laws was incremental. Yet, every action required a reaction, which was understandably slow to come from the Jewish community. The latter was at first not terribly interested, well-informed, or motivated.

In the early years of Hitler's ascendancy only a very few had the vision and foresight to act, to rally their nuclear and extended family, turn their non-liquid assets into cash and leave Germany, with their treasure, their family, their welfare and their sanity intact.

As the previous a chapter discussed, a rift had formed in the Jewish community on the matter of emigration. Pulling up roots and leaving like the proverbial "wandering Jew" after generations of life in Germany could not have been deemed easy. Giving up one's business or profession to start again in distant, unknown lands, say, at middle age must have seemed like a momentous decision. And, how about the older generation . . . aging parents and grandparents or beloved uncles and aunts? What would be their fate in the "new country" . . . or—worse yet—if left behind? These were torturous decisions. And, what about the "new country"? My father must have thought about these factors: How will we live . . . without money . . . where everything is new and different—the people, the culture, the laws . . . how will I protect my young son? To face all these huge question marks—and more—led to the need for macro decision-making. Perhaps—for some—it was just too soon to make these difficult life and death decisions. The insecurity of change can be overwhelming.

My father, it seems, was not in a hurry. His inaction of the first three or four years under Nazi rule was understandable. He was greatly influenced by the anti-emigration camp, especially his new uncles, the family patriarchs. In the meantime, his country's government had disenfranchised him and every other Jew in the country. But, wasn't Germany (the nation he fought for in uniform in World War One) still recognized internationally among the civilized nations of the world and awarded the 1936 Olympics? And indeed what an event it was! It was a show case for the New Germany, yes, the new Nazi Germany. It was one big party for the Fuehrer, for Fascism, for dictators everywhere on the planet, for re-armament, for militarism, for the successful alliance of big business and the old aristocracy, and for the birth of an evil empire. But, the world looked away. It was OK to degrade black athletes and kick Jewish athletes off the team. It was a vulgar exhibit of nationalism run amuck, complete with an over-the-top, in-your-face display of massed giant-sized streaming banners and flags everywhere saying: "Look at the Swastika . . . look at it . . . look at it now . . . for it will soon fly everywhere. It symbolizes the new Aryan age of the Germanic *Uebermensch.* Listen world! . . . We are preparing to conquer you under your very own eyes."

And did the assembled nations of the world wake up and take notice? Quite to the contrary. Although the threat was anything but subtle, the world was asleep, exhausted by severe economic depression and political upheaval everywhere. The German people were conveniently on cruise control. Their silence equated to acquiescence.

Fascism acquired legitimacy. Mussolini was dancing the jig to his own beat long before Hitler. In America, Roosevelt had great difficulties in ending the Great Depression. Fascist opportunism was rearing its ugly head in America as well. Without public uproar or complaint, anti-Semitism increased exponentially. Jewish-American leaders took cover. In Great Britain, fascism took even bigger and more serious strides. If one is not a voracious reader, perhaps you saw the movie "Remains of the Day" and recall the Fascist aristocrats entertaining their fellow-travelers in their black shirts and bespoke Old Bond Street suits, plus Nazi bigwigs from the Reich. They partied and plotted. They ate in the grand and ornate dining room while they committed treason against their country. They planned to incite disorder and overthrow the government. They planned to incite *ueber*-anti-Semitism. They drank the last brandy of the evening as a toast to their own New Order under the banner of Fascism. Have we all conveniently forgotten that chapter of history? And in the meantime, who defended Democracy? Luckily, in America, F.D.R. did in the best way he could: give a little here, make a concession there, bend a little, but do not break. With the advent of the New Deal, it can be said with certainty that with all his warts and blemishes, he saved America from Fascism, Communism, and/or revolution, and in the last analysis from economic and financial ruin. But who defended the Jews? Who defended my father? Nazi-Germany fooled the world. Could it not fool its own people, including its Jews?

My dear father faced a dilemma, a cruel riddle that he could not solve. He was an excellent salesman and businessman, who had married into the Strauss family business. Having married my mother in 1933, he was just settling into the business in 1934, when he had to deal with the rather sudden and untimely death of his father-in-law, my maternal grandfather. He took over the running of the company. There were now two families to feed. He focused on the business, made positive changes and greatly modernized the firm. The business grew and prospered.

Unfortunately, the cruel events in Germany overtook him—and many more Jews—like a tsunami might overrun a doomed Indonesian coastal village. Bam! . . . and it was *Kristallnacht*, November 9, 1938. He was unceremoniously arrested in our home and carted off to Dachau where he was beaten and tortured. He returned to us in January of 1939; but he returned a broken man. They were all broken men . . . those unfortunate victims. Dachau was a subjective awareness and experience of horror, from which a neurological fingerprint remained forever. My father was never ever the same man again.

As previously reported, the next major hurdle came in 1942. As you will recall, my father was interned in a Vichy-French minimum security labor camp near Marseille. He worked in the office. His work, his management—and organizational skills impressed the camp commandant . . . and they became "friends". My father was permitted regular and frequent weekend passes to come see my mother and me in Marseille. As the Nazis intensified their internment and transport of Jews in both sectors of France, the camp commandant warned my father. When he left for Marseille that warm August Saturday morning, the commandant advised him not to return. Upon father's arrival in Marseille, he briefed my mother at once. Mother was very excited and immediately saw an opportunity to save her beloved husband's life. She begged him not to return under any circumstance. She told him that she would whisk him off to our country hideout that very day. His reply was non-committal. He correctly pointed out that his escape may put mother and me in greater danger. The clamor of terror invaded his psyche. Fear of social things is different from fear of physical things. It is much harder to avoid social fears. Due to the continuum of the trauma over these momentous and horrendous years, had he lost his grip on his fearfulness? Was he trapped in an endless loop of what-ifs? Could he still deal with the brain circuitry of flight or fight? He said he would make up his mind in the morning. On Sunday, at the usual time, he left. His action was merely the dutiful return to the very circumstances of his imprisoned existence. He could not outrun his own nature and his inner-directed thoughts and feelings. Who can really say what his thoughts were at this point in time? Like many others, he had no training or preparation for the decision he had to make while chaos and insanity ruled the earth.

We never saw him again. The now lengthy internment, the terrible fate of his aged parents under his very own eyes, a present and a future that was now beyond anyone's clear comprehension continued to undermine his mindset. The last two communications my mother and I ever received from my father are two letters. (Exh.) They are vaguely other-worldly . . . excruciatingly sad and disturbing. The first letter was sent to mother on the day he returned to the camp. Father—and his fellow Jewish internees were advised that they were about to be "transferred". This letter was restlessly followed by another the very next day. His tone was now subdued, full of weary sadness, and fatalistic denial.

Temperament is a complex, multilayered thing. It explains normal human variation. As with the anti-emigrationist family elders and patriarchs, it had to do with a root problem, an irrationality, a calamitous and unreasonable inner logic that defines the human condition. In this sad case it led to ruinous results, which devastated my dear mother—and me—but not forever.

After all that immeasurable sadness, however, my father's good name, his character, his spirit, the very essence of his being has always been with me . . . and remains as such. To his critics—if there are any—I strongly say for him, "Walk a mile in my shoes . . . or shut up!" As for my esteemed father, permit me to add that uncertainty has a nasty way of making us conjure up the very worst possibilities. That's when the hellish hand-wringing, hyperbole, and hubris come into play. I never subscribed to that game. My father's never-ending presence survived. It looks over my shoulder as I write these lines. The Nazis robbed him of his life, and in so doing the voice to explain (not defend)! While this book will never be a New York Times Best Seller, it is the place to stand in his stead as his advocate, and thereby give him some semblance of justice. The outcome was sad for us all. However, my mother and I live out good lives in a free and democratic land. His grandchildren and great-grandchildren and untold generations will, hopefully, do the same. To be sure it is a legacy attributable to my mother and me, but also to my wonderful father. We make the best decisions we can whilst the future is hidden from our eyes. Success has many fathers. But let us not forget him who gave up so much. To fail him now in my writings would amount to becoming a latent accomplice to the heinous system that murdered him. I will not forget! We will never know the real answers; but my long view—after all these years—put me squarely in the corner of a gentleman and a gentle man who bore and faced a terrible burden while the ones he loved most survived, prospered and gave birth to new generations. The memories of my dearest father have become a "sacred" story for me. As such, the Nazi bastards failed, for his spirit is alive and with me every day.

CHAPTER 14

Victory. But, The Journey Continues.

1944-1945-1946

All of my mother's illnesses went away in the beautiful, healthy, invigorating mountain air of Montana. Her frequent, lingering colds, her bronchitis, her kidney and her eye problems were most likely caused and aggravated by the stress before she came to this resort area. She thrived in the natural beauty and relative calm of this atmosphere. She came to visit me and the Neuburgers in St. Gallen regularly and frequently, and I continued to visit her at least twice a year. And, what a delicious reunion that was each and every time. She was pleased with the administration of the camp. She felt useful in her work, and she became very close to her friends. Communal life can be instrumental in forming the closest of bonds.

As for me, 1944 saw me promoted to the fourth grade and a new teacher. Whereas Kindergarten through Third Grade was at a nearby coed school, was still relatively easy and easy-going—even nurturing—the fourth year was boys-only and serious business. The fourth year, or the continuation of elementary school, began a cluster of three years, one classroom, one teacher. He taught all subjects, including gym. The school was, by all standards, quite far away. However, it was directly opposite the Neuburger factory and office. Most of the boys in my class came from another school. New friendships would have to be forged. This was not necessarily an easy task at this age and stage. There were two Jewish boys in my class. The first was Harry Richter, the son of the obligatory Jewish dentist in town. At first, Harry approached the situation gingerly. Although the entire Neuburger family, including me, was a client of his father, he did not wish to risk guilt by association.

However, he did eventually come around. We alternated playing at each other's homes. Nevertheless, after I left Switzerland in 1946, despite my many returns, I never socialized with Harry again. The other Jew in the class was a *Kindertransport* child to whom the Steiner family provided a temporary home. He left as soon as the war ended. Although we also played regularly, I never saw him again. I wish I could remember his name.

Herr Nuesch, our teacher, was a handsome, erect, healthy looking man in his early-to-mid-forties. First impression: This is a no-nonsense guy. He proved to be a good, yet demanding, but also fair teacher. He was an excellent athlete, the equivalent of a state champion in gymnastics in his earlier years, and his conduct of gym class often struck the most awful fear into me, for this was an activity I would never excel in. Excel? . . . My performance wasn't even satisfactory. But somehow, he understood, and he and I went about finding a way around all that.

The Swiss school system, at this grade level, supplied a mid-morning snack, the core of which was the daily glass of milk. I abhorred milk; it actually sickened me. And so, Aunt Selma had to provide a note which permitted me **not** to have milk. If these two problems were to be the only major challenges, then I could consider myself quite lucky, really. My good friend Heinz, who lived just two blocks away, transferred to the St. Leonhardtschule on St. Leonhardt Strasse with me. So, there was one friend, and someone to share the long walk to school. Ah, but here was the rub! School started at 8 AM. The Neuburger factory and office across the street started at 7AM. Now, if I chose to arise one hour early and leave with Hanns on his army-issue motor cycle, there would not be a walk to school, but a thrilling ride instead . . . and that became the routine. The exception came when Hanns was on required active duty reserve stints. He was a messenger in the army, hence the possession of a motor cycle. In the Swiss army reserve, one takes home all equipment, including weapons . . . and motor cycles. Good system. Later, he even got a side car. That meant my friend Heinz could also hitch a ride. He was overjoyed. I guess that made up for the times that he had to walk while I rode to school, which in fact could easily have resulted in a serious question for The Ethicist. But, Heinz was a laid back sort of guy, typically Swiss. I guess life presented him with far more important and far larger challenges and joys. And besides, I often walked home with him, so that we could spend some time at play, after we had both done our home work.

And so life and school and cub scouts and religious education and services and my time with the Neuburgers went on in an easy-to-take routine that seemed to satisfy my immediate needs. Because of my unique transportation situation, I spent a lot of time at the Neuburger firm. Be it before school or after, I would first find an empty desk and do my homework. Then, I would ask for something to do, which would often be some easy task in the office. Or, I might help the apprentice in the piece goods department, a mere girl of only sixteen or seventeen, in giving out the cloth to be cut in the factory. She was a great gal, who would stay on with the firm and forge an excellent career for herself. I would get to know everybody in the firm, from the office to the factory. Finding a new chore for me became more and more difficult. Then, Uncle David had a great idea. As manufacturers of ladies' blouses, dresses and suits, the company used a lot of cloth covered buttons. They were made by one of the apprentice girls in the factory. This job was now assigned to me. I was paid a penny per button. Uncle David soon commented in jest that if all his supplies cost him as much as his buttons, he would soon be out of business. I loved being at the plant. I'm quite certain that the seeds for my future career were sown at this point.

The year 1944, June to be precise, was to be the year that changed so many things. Thanks to the Russian Army and Allied victories all over the globe, the direction of the war was changing. As soon as the American and British troops landed on the beaches of France, a huge map went up in Hanns' office. Our new "hobby" became following the Allies' progress and changing the little color-coded stickpins every day. There was a new atmosphere everywhere. Hope and optimism was the order of the day. I believe it even changed relationships. I felt more at ease in school and among the other boys.

I began to feel that perhaps I belonged in this place. Another matter that helped me to feel more comfortable was the sudden beginning of massive, day-time Allied bombing of German cities. Huge sorties of Allied, mostly American, bombers started flying through Swiss air space en route to their targets. As a precaution, the Swiss government sounded the alarm every time these planes reached the air space over Swiss cities. The schools' operating procedure was as follows. Children living near the schools or those having access to any shelter near the school were to take three or four classmates to this location and proceed to the cellar of the building. I took my friend, Heinz, and two other of my class "favorites" across the street to the Neuburger firm. We went to the cellar the first time, and then never again. We found a place to play in the office area and waited for the sirens to give the all-clear. These almost daily interludes greatly helped me cement my relationship with classmates. In my spare time, I began playing soccer with them and others in the park that surrounded the school. For the first time, I was invited to their homes . . . and vice versa. Our annual school field trips and travels became a pleasurable activity. Suddenly, the pressure was off. How the schools could operate under these conditions became a puzzle to me . . . and to the adults. Once the all-clear sirens sounded, it took considerable time to reassemble the pupils and resume instruction. Perhaps by that time it would be near the two-hour lunch break. It was not unusual for the planes to return in the afternoon, after they had dropped their bombs. And, so it went on until the end of the war. We youngsters got a huge kick not only out of the reduced school hours, but also out of the knowledge that this massive concentration of air power would inflict great damage and hasten the defeat of the Nazis. We would look to the skies in wonderment. The sky would turn black with airplanes in tight formations. Everyone's morale was up one hundred percent. Bonus: fewer gym classes.

At Camp Montana, Mother and her fellow internees where overwhelmed by the same feelings of joy and hope. The end was in sight. The atmosphere brightened. The anti-Semitic camp administrators were forced to lighten up on their act. Although the Swiss remained strictly neutral, their pro-Allies leanings could now be aired. Switzerland would remain a democratic republic. There would be no *Anschluss* here. Mother was able to visit me and my foster family more often. And—most importantly—it was a time to think . . . think about the future . . . now that there was a future.

*   *   *

In the meantime, the Nazi's began to realize that in all likelihood *this* war would not be won. So, they turned their attention to the other war—the war against European Jewry.

The all-out effort to eradicate our people became Priority One. The mass murder of innocent Jewish men, women and children had even become an occasion for "Festivals", especially in Poland, where 42,000 Jews were killed over one such weekend "celebration". The Auschwitz complex had become a vast instrument of mass murder. It consisted of thirty sub-camps. Jews were now shipped to Auschwitz from Vienna and Budapest and Rome and Athens.

While brave Americans are climbing up the cliffs above the beaches of Normandy, Auschwitz-Birkenau records its highest ever *daily* number of Jews gassed and burned at just over 9000. Six huge pits are used to burn the bodies, as the number now exceeds the capacity of the crematories.

Unprecedented murder and war crimes now becomes the growth industry in a country about to be turned to rubble by the American Air Force.

However, Hitler—and his inner circles of fanatic cretins—is unperturbed. He orders Eichman to proceed to Hungary at once. His orders are to "assist those malingering Hungarian puppet officials" in their duty to cooperate in rounding up the remaining Jewish population immediately. Hitler uses his panzers to lay siege to the Hungarian parliament. He fears that Hungary may seek a separate peace with Russia. In Amsterdam, the Gestapo arrests Anne Frank and her family and ships them to Auschwitz. Anne and her sister Margot are later transferred to the concentration camp at Bergen-Belsen, where Anne dies of typhus three weeks before the German surrender.

*   *   *

For my mother the imminent prospect of peace presented a bittersweet scenario. Did her beloved husband, my dear father, survive so far? Would he survive for the remainder of the war? And, how about all the other valued relatives? But, perhaps the most important question became what to do after the war ended. For my mother, there was no question, no doubt, no debate. Her one and only plan was to renew the effort to emigrate to America. It was her total focus to reunite with her dearest and closest relatives. She contacted the Erlangers once again. They, you will recall, were our American relatives whose 1938 Affidavit was still on record. They replied in the affirmative with the promptness that wartime postal service would permit. In their reply, Milton and Sydney Erlanger added that the families of two other cousins would join in the sponsorship arrangements as a sign of family solidarity and as a thankful tribute to the survivors. They also volunteered to pay for the passage to America for us, Alfred and for any other survivors of the immediate family.

The Neuburgers were, of course, instantly ready and prepared to seriously and constructively discuss all aspects of emigration and immigration with mother. Foremost they held out the possibility and opportunity for my mother and me to remain in Switzerland. Mother's employment in the firm would not be a problem. Mother's opportunity to set up an independent household for herself, her son, and hopefully her husband would be encouraged and facilitated. Counting on their connections, the chance at Swiss citizenship—after eight or ten years—was not discounted. The Neuburgers were well aware of what thoughts my mother was thinking and what feelings she was harboring deep-down in her heart. They knew full well that my mother's unwavering intention was to join her family and relatives in New York. However, it was a prerequisite for the Neuburgers—acting totally in character—to once again show their collective concern, sensitivity and immense generosity to offer an alternative. Friends of the Neuburgers, committed Zionists, even offered the idea of our settling in Israel, all expenses paid plus a generous stipend for the assimilation years. Thanks, but no thanks was of course mother's reply. Mother was fortunate that Uncle David was still alive during this crucial time. He would act and proceed in the most rational manner, with my mother's interests and future welfare uppermost in his mind. He correctly insisted that my mother could not entertain emigration plans to America without attaining some skills to earn a living. The entire Neuburger family agreed, as did my mother. The obvious plan was for mother to learn a trade immediately after her discharge from Camp Montana, or perhaps even sooner. Naturally, the needle trade was the most opportune. And, so my mother would learn how to sew.

However, the Allied military conquest took considerably longer than anticipated immediately after the landings on the beaches of Normandy. Those colored stickpins on Hanns' map moved far too slowly to the north and to the east. When the surprising news of the Battle of the Bulge hit the radio and the newspapers, we—and all of Europe—held our collective breaths. Those thousand-bomber formations suddenly didn't seem as formidable and invincible as before. Doubt and fear returned. Would the war in Europe drag on to some unthinkable stalemate a la World War One? Fortunately, the bravery of America's fighting men and women reversed the situation, and progress continued along the Western Front. Pushing forward to the *Siegfried* Line and to the Rhein, in other words the Allies' attempts to cross the German border from the west, once again proved to be difficult and brutally bloody. It slowed down progress—and victory—once again. However, that too passed. America's fighting machine had simply become too strong and determined. It would not be deterred from smashing Hitler and his Third Reich. America and its allies demanded unconditional surrender . . . and on May 7, 1945 it came.

*   *   *

Once the war had ended, my mother's top priority was to immerse herself into a frantic determination of whether my father was dead or alive and the subsequent search for my father. Until the Red Cross, the new hastily-formed displaced persons organizations, the Jewish agencies, etc.,

etc., got organized and set up throughout Europe, this task was anything but easy. But mother, always the overachiever, ever the pioneer, tried various shortcuts, alas without success. She contacted individuals with whom she had contact during the war. She simply would not relinquish nor give up hope. It became known that concentration camps liberated by the Russians were quickly emptied. Sadly and inexplicably many of the inmates shipped to Siberia. The stories and rumors were infinite and took on a life of their own. Mother's attempts to find my father continued into 1947, when we were already living in America.

My mother finally realized that she must shift priorities and focus on our exodus from Switzerland. Fortunately, there was no hurry. She soon found out that civilian transport to America would be extremely difficult. All passenger ships were being used to transfer troops to the Pacific Theater of War, where the battle against the Japanese continued to rage. Two nuclear weapons later, it ended as well. However, ships remained in great demand by the armed forces. Battle-weary G.I.'s, and members of all the services, some of whom had not seen their families for three or four years, had to be shipped home. Replacements and materiel had to be ferried to all the ports of the newly-occupied locations. In Germany, a large occupation force would remain for ten years. After that, in 1955, western allied forces were renamed *Gasttruppen*, "guest troops" and would remain as a shield against the U.S.S.R. Germany and its The New German Army joined NATO. A relatively small American force remains to this very day.

For my mother and me the point was that in late 1945 and mid-1946 there were simply no ships available for civilian passengers. The planning proceeded anyway. Mother almost welcomed the opportunity to get in more needle work training. She applied for vocational training in garment cutting at the local O.R.T. school. This application had to be approved by the Swiss Federal Bureau of Justice—and Police. Permission was granted on the basis of mother's pledge to leave Switzerland on the first available transport. (Exh.) The fact that the O.R.T is a world-wide, Jewish, non-governmental, charitable organization did not seem to faze the Swiss bureaucrats at all.

The Neuburgers arranged for me to start English lessons with a tutor. All this hectic planning activity was just a bit overwhelming for me, as I evaluated the entire situation as a two-edged sword once again. Certainly I understood my mother's plan. However, for me America meant Country Number Five in a time span of just over eleven years. It meant once again a new language, new school, new people, new culture . . . and no roots, no protection, no money. I was just beginning to feel really comfortable with my schoolmates and my friends. I was included in their games and activities. I had long ago mastered the difficult Swiss-German dialect. No Swiss citizen would have been able to single me out as a "foreigner" . . . or "*etranger*" as they still say in the sad musical, "Cabaret", that perfectly crafted tale of pre-war Nazi Germany. And, there were other problems in paradise. The long awaited, but now permanent, arrival of my mother in St. Gallen would cause occasional friction between my mother and Aunt Selma. Nothing major ever erupted because—after all—they were both extraordinary "ladies". However, sometimes struggling to maintain her reserve and her character, mother wisely refrained from any escalation. There were no damaged sensibilities, no false expectations. *Noise* never trumped *meaning* . . . at least not that I can remember now as memory has become withered nostalgia. As for me, nevertheless, I did at times feel the pull and tug between two "Mothers" and the somewhat complicated visceral relationship. I remained taciturn.

In summary, I am quite certain it was all meant well, and there is no need to examine it microscopically in these pages. Now that my mother was a part of the Neuburger household, Anneliese came to visit on weekends even more regularly. She and my mother got along famously. They shared the guest room and often talked long into the night. Anneliese's sense of humor could bridge any discomfort. She could easily buffer a tense situation. Also not exactly helping the occasional all-around stress that occurs in any household was the fact that Hedi had to leave as Wally was once again permitted to work for the Neuburgers . . . or work for Jews, that is.

Finally, in the late Spring of 1946, the Erlangers decided that enough was enough. They sent to my mother airplane tickets for two from London to New York, with prior stops in Nice and Paris. In those days, there was only first class. What a splendid adventure that would be. Those tickets certainly and suddenly speeded up all preparations. Mother planned our trip to France and England. My English lessons were intensified. The Neuburgers supplied my mother and me with new clothes. Mother had to secure all the necessary documents. Swiss bureaucracy even required the approval of mother's packing list by the State/Canton of St. Gallen; cost—per stamp—40 Swiss cents (less than a U.S. dime). (Exh.) However and perhaps most importantly, how—and from whom—does a stateless person obtain potentially trouble-free travel documents? For this specific purpose, and in defense of their bureaucracy, the Swiss had an excellent system. (Exh.) Our targeted departure date from St. Gallen was set for July 23, 1946. A final vacation outing in several cars was planned for family and friends, including my mother, Aunt Selma, Hanns, Walter and his girl-friend-de-jour, and of course my "girl friend", Marion and her grandparents. Great pictures! (Exh.) For now, there were many goodbyes to be said: Aunt Martha and her family, separately Anneliese and the other relatives and friends of the Neuburgers who had spoiled me these many years. Add to that list my teachers, boy scout and religious leaders, and—of course—my fellow pupils, my playmates and my close friends. However, the inevitable day had to come, the day to say goodbye to everyone and everything.

The parting date with the Neuburgers was happily and enjoyably given two days' grace in that Aunt Selma, Hanns and Walter accompanied us to Geneva. We spent these two lovely bonus days and nights together at the shore of its beautiful lake and the surrounding mountains of the Jura and the Alps. Aunt Selma was in tears the entire time. She already blamed herself for letting us go into an uncharted future in an unknown land over 3000 miles away. The final goodbye came at Cornavin Airport, as we boarded the plane for Nice. Just one more wave. Just one last wave. I could not look back again. Mother was, of course, in tears. The plane taxied and took off. The Neuburgers, still waving, disappeared from our view. My ambivalent feelings about leaving Switzerland returned that very second. It was July 25, 1946.

*   *   *

We had a wonderful time in Nice, as described in the previous chapter. Unfortunately, there was no reason to go to Marseille. The Eichberg family, who were so good to us during the war, was wiped out in its entirety, all deported and murdered by the Nazis. With great sadness in our hearts, we then proceeded to Lyon by train, to visit the Kahn family, headed by Raff, the Jewish French Army Colonel, who had also been so immensely helpful during our crisscrossing of wartime France. Here the news was better. The entire family survived. No member of the immediate family (wife, children and his aging parents) were ever arrested. The visit, as would be the case over and over, was emotional: A celebration of the survivors . . . sadness and mourning for the good friends who did not survive. The Kahn story illustrates once more the influence of the Resistance in unoccupied France, and to some extent at least must be weighed against serious and accurate charges of French cooperation with the Nazis. Generally, however, there was great relief that the war over. No one celebrated that event better than the French. That certain *joie de vivre* was in the air once again. It was summer, the streets and the cafes were filled with people. Yet, things were far from normal in France. There were shortages of all kinds. France was to face yet another difficult winter. However, everyone understood the value of renewed independence and freedom. Reconstruction of cities and towns was widely required. Scores would have to be settled and resettled. The French people, now divided by the specter of wartime collaboration, would have to work it out. Some would be punished. Some would be falsely accused. Some of the guilty would not be punished at all. Life would go on.

From Lyon, mother and I went to Paris by train, to visit mother's Montana roommate and great friend, Margot Schott. Margot had lived in Paris before the war and chose to return there in 1945. Margot was an attractive woman, a few years younger than my mother. Her husband, who was also in Montana of course, was said to be impotent, and they agreed to an open marriage. Margot had lots of friends! She was now divorced. It seemed to my mother that she had easily slipped back into the Paris lifestyle. Paris, physically untouched by the Nazis, was simply overwhelming to us in its size and its immense beauty and liveliness. This huge urban area, cosmopolitan and sophisticated, was "a first" for my mother and me. St. Gallen and its population of 60,000, was after all a back-water "village" compared to this great and wondrous city. And the comparison to Mannheim (population 225,000 at the start of the war), contrary to my mother's sentimental assessment of the city of her birth and youth, was not that much different. But then, how many cities in the world can compare favorably with Paris? Headed for London and New York, we would soon find out.

London. The difficult lives of the Lowenbergs during the war was discussed at length in a previous chapter. My mother and I were delighted to see them. Of course, they and especially Aunt Dorothy (formerly Dora) had to slowly and surely accept the fact that my father, Aunt Dora's beloved older brother, was no longer alive. Aunt Dora recounted the wonderful life he and she had as children, teenagers and young adults, memories now and forever clouded by the events of the Holocaust. However, sooner rather than later, we all mercifully realized that our reunion symbolized a certain victory, a celebration of life and survival. And so, we vowed to spend a few great days together in this second overwhelming city that was London. A strange thing happened in London. I totally refused to speak English. Lessons to the contrary, I would not speak a word of English. Be it on the streets, in the subway and buses, in restaurants, in the movies, I steadfastly, and without giving any sound reasons, refused to speak even a word of English. Now, this was rather painful to our relatives. The British, having suffered greatly from German aggression, humiliation, and death over six wartime years, did not exactly "cotton to" hearing German spoken in their midst. However fervently my relatives appealed to my better nature, their plea was unsuccessful. Was this some kind of protest over having to leave Switzerland? Was this some expression of fear in view of having to face a new life once again? Probably a little of both. Nevertheless, a fine time was had by all, for after all, we knew that we would soon celebrate another reunion with the Lowenbergs in New York. They planned to arrive in New York the following year.

*   *   *

While in London, we received two letters from both Aunt Selma and Hanns. These letters also survived in their original form amongst my mother's stuff. Both letters were written on personalized black-bordered stationery, as Aunt Selma was still grieving over the loss of her husband, our beloved Uncle David. The first letter is dated August 8th, 1946, two weeks after our tearful departure from Geneva. The second letter is dated a week later, August 15th. It should be of special note that Hanns, still a very young man now twenty-four years old, writes that he will continue to be an active partner in the continuation and furtherance of the special relationship between our families.

The letters appear here in translation.

Letter dated August 8th.

> *"Meine Lieben,"* (My dear ones.)

> "We were very happy to receive your telegram and then speak to you on the telephone. You are now reunited with your loved ones, your dear mother and grandmother and her dear sister-in-law. We are especially glad to hear that Alfred was able to see them earlier in the year. I can just imagine your mutual joy. We miss you very much. It will be difficult to replace your presence with us. We can only hope that our reunion with you will be sooner rather than later." Aunt Selma then states that she is increasingly worried about the rapid deterioration of her sister's heart problems and general health. She then comments on the doctor's efforts, and after exhorting G-d's help for a steady recovery, she adds: "You dear Kate became very close to my sister and know how frail she has become." And refers to her as "your Aunt Friedl". She continues: "And you, dear Ernstl (not a typo), how did you like the "'preview flight'" to Nice? Did it agree with

you? Was it difficult for you all to leave your dear ones after such
a short visit? I will try to visit them in the not-too-distant future.
How was your reunion with your loved ones is London? How
are they? All our mutual friends and relatives here in Switzerland
have asked about you and send their best and sincerest regards,
especially Marion and her grandmother. In closing, we lovingly
place our arms around you and hug you with our sincerest love
and regard." Hanns, in his usual breezy, yet sincere manner,
repeats most of these sentiments, and promises to write more
the next time.

Letter dated August 15th.
This letter is considerably longer.

"Your lovely, thorough and comprehensive letter, expected
with great anticipation, is herewith gratefully acknowledged. It
expresses so well your all-around joy in—at long last—seeing all
your loved ones. We are so very happy for you, and continue to
hope that these feelings will continue, especially after your big
journey, where a happy future clearly appears before you in the
land of freedom. We will always stand behind you in the event
you should be disappointed, and life does not turn out to be what
you so dearly hope and wish for. In the meantime, we believe
that you will collect almost overwhelming impressions from all
directions that will surely be your inspiration.

You, dear Ernstl, seem to have fallen in love with Paris. How
do you like London? I can certainly understand that you and the
Lowenbergs had a grand reunion and are enjoying some happy
days together. Sadly, I can also understand the pain, the grief
and sadness that is brought on by the fact that an all-important
member of the family is missing. We must, nevertheless, thank
G-d that you have all survived and find yourselves reunited. On
the other hand, dear Kate, your departure has left me with a
huge void. I have great difficulties gathering my thoughts." With
considerable sadness, Aunt Selma writes about her sister's relapse
and hospitalization, this time at a hospital in Zurich, where a
top heart specialist will examine and treat her. "Nevertheless,
she remembered to send her best regards to you both. You can
imagine", she continues, "just how worried, broken-hearted and

generally distressed I am on this very weekend that marks one year (on the Jewish calendar) since my dear husband passed away." Actually exhibiting the stress, she then gets lost in minutia, but quickly recovers and writes about her two sons. "I spoke to Walter. He is in Ascona on a short vacation. He reports that his studies are very demanding. However, he is very happy and content. Hanns is very busy at work. I suspect that he will be the first one in the family to see you again. Our distant relative, Walter Brandeis from America, who is currently visiting us, has invited Hanns to America. I have the feeling that Hanns will not wait too long to make such a trip. Let me have your London telephone number, as I would like to speak to you before you leave for America." Again after some more minutia, she continues "Dear Ernstli, Marion misses you very much and yearns for you. [How about that sports fans?] Other news from St. Gallen: The new cantor has started and we already wish we had Cantor Neufeld back. His voice was much better than the new one's. However, the latter sweats more!' After more minutia she very kindly and directly addresses Aunt Dora ("*Liebe* Dora"), in the hope to see her before she and her family also moves to America. After all, Dora was the niece—by the latter's marriage—of Aunt Selma's brother, the husband of Aunt Martha. Returning to mother's attention and mine, she concludes "My dear ones, you are constantly in my thoughts. I send to you my greetings and my kisses. Your Aunt Selma." Hanns adds some very personal and kind words and admits he just wants to schmooze a little. "The entire firm", he continues "sends their best regards to you, Ernst, with special regards from "you know who"!! [Yeah, I know who: That wonderful young lady in the piece goods department.] They all wish you a pleasant and safe flight across the big pond. I join them in these best of wishes. I guess your next letter will be from America. In the meantime, all the best to all of you."

These letters were of immense meaning and personal value to my mother and me. They respectfully and warmly addressed us as real and closest of family. They sound as if we had known each other intimately all our lives. The Neuburgers were not just generous distant relatives or friends. They were surrogate parents and brothers. They helped to raise me. Their largesse towards my dear mother was exemplary. They accepted us both into their inner family circle. This is a very precious life experience. And it is important for our grandchildren to know and understand how very blessed we were and are by this affiliation. You can see now, dear reader, why and how this relationship grew deeper and deeper, ever more meaningfully, and actively survives to this very day.

CHAPTER 15

America—Part I

1946-1949

On August 20, 1946, American Overseas Airline's flight no. 51/20 to New York's LaGuardia Airport took off from London Airport. The total flight—and ground-time was scheduled to be twenty-three hours. There would be two scheduled refueling stops: First in Shannon, Ireland, where a lovely meal was served in the dining room. Irish linen products, Irish whiskey, souvenirs and all sorts of other duty-free bargains were available for sale. Then, after the long nighttime crossing through the skies over the North Atlantic, the plane was scheduled to land in Newfoundland, the Canadian province. As the locals might say, a proper English breakfast was served while the plane was being refueled for the long flight south along the eastern seaboard. For hours and hours one flies over the dense forestation that is Canada. Today's non-stop jet flights from Europe to the northeastern United States still fly this exact same route.

Aboard were Kate Feibelmann (soon to be spelled with one "n") and her son Ernst (soon to be spelled and pronounced Ernest). The flight would be a novel, exciting, exclusive and luxurious experience. However, as for the duty-free bargains, only a few post cards and stamps were within Kate's meager financial means. Luckily, she still had some British coins left in her pocket, for surely she did not want to break those few $20 bills in her purse. They were her only financial assets. Future "luxury" would have to wait. (Before leaving Switzerland, Kate still had a few gold coins left. She gave them to Aunt Selma as a small, symbolic token of gratitude for the Neuburger family's immense generosity.)

Throughout the flight Kate was extremely excited and upbeat. This was her dream-come-true: A decisive break with the "old", and for her, an optimistic, hopeful start of the "new life". She could hardly wait to see the most important part of the family: her uncles, aunts and cousins. The very thought of America and the great metropolis, New York, ran through her very being like a powerful stimulant. I, on the other hand, was far more subdued, and once again somewhat anxious and scared. I believe that the London "language strike" had said it all.

At approximately three o'clock in the afternoon, the plane landed at La Guardia, at that time the only commercial airport serving the New York metropolitan area. This was still an era of light commercial air traffic. There was no circling in the air or waiting for an available runway or a gate. There were no lines at customs or immigration. And so, without delay, my mother and I were in the airport reception area. We realized that at long last the ground and earth below our firmly planted feet were a part of New York City and—more importantly—America! Mother was flush with the thrill that comes upon the accomplishment of a long-hoped-for wish and goal and dream. So demonstrably pleased was she that I thought she would kneel down and kiss this genuine American soil. And, perhaps she would have if Cousin Martha—obviously the family's designated greeter—had not called out to us . . . and waved . . . and jumped up and down a bit. Hugs and kisses all around, and off to the waiting taxis.

Now, Cousin Martha, as I learned later, was not really the type to jump up and down too frequently. This was Martha Schloss, a certified member of the Haas Clan, who along with her husband and two sons, had used our 1937 Affidavit to come to the United States. She would play an extremely important role in the early years of Kate's (and Ernest's) life in New York. For Martha, the cab fare probably topped any such budget item for the entire year. However, with our heavy luggage, there was little choice . . . and besides that, we were the first post-war refugees of the family to arrive in New York. Hence, we deserved a little bit of "special treatment'. And yes, there would be others to follow us. The cab headed westward through the borough of Queens . . . and soon there it was: the world-famous skyline, complete with its symbolic attraction, the Empire State Building, majestically representing America's strength and wealth and recent victory over the evil ex-empires on the planet. Can you imagine the impression it made on an eleven-year-old boy? My mother also glowed with excitement and satisfaction. Crossing the Queensboro Bridge, the cab headed for the upper West Side . . . "way upper", as we were to learn later.

The master plan was for mother and me to live with Uncle Ferdinand and Aunt Alice, at least for a while. Yes, the same Ferdinand Haas you read about in a previous chapter. He and his wife, and at times his daughter, lived at 87 Hamilton Place at the corner of 139th Street. Hamilton Place is a short street, diagonally connecting Broadway (from 136th Street) to Amsterdam Avenue (at 144th Street). It is at the very edge of Harlem, Amsterdam Avenue being the dividing line. Of course, as the cab pulled up to the apartment house, we had absolutely no idea or the slightest knowledge of any of these "logistics". We took the elevator up to the third floor. Martha had the key to the apartment. We went inside and waited for my mother's uncle and aunt to return from work. It was just about that time . . . and then the New Life for the Feibelmans, sadly, tragically sans Leon, would begin in earnest.

My initial impression: The apartment was extremely small. Although the living room faced the 139th Street, the apartment was depressingly dark. After all, there was an almost identical apartment building casting its long, dark shadow across the narrow, treeless street. And, it was hot! It was August in New York, August in America, where temperatures and humidity reach heights never experienced in Switzerland. It was the age before air-conditioning. And, all the windows were closed. Where is my mansion now? . . . my huge, cool rooms, my huge windows, my high ceilings, my green, spectacular view? This is worse than my worst nightmare, albeit, it is almost exactly what I imagined and feared. This is my "new life"? When is the next plane back to my old life? Help!

Snap out of it Feibelman—with the one "n"—I heard my own voice saying. And then, suddenly: 'It will be alright. Mother Kate is still at the helm, and—arguably—she has not failed you yet.' At any rate, my impressions—at least for that moment in time—are not important. This book, after all, is all about my mother. And in any event, mercifully, I could hear a key turn, and Aunt Alice walked in the door. Uncle Ferdinand would arrive just minutes after her.

It was another one of those priceless reunions: tearful, joyful, hopeful. There continued to be a visible transformation in my mother's mood. While she should have felt exhausted and tired from the trip and the overwhelming new experiences, she was radiant, energized, bubbling over with the best of thoughts and feelings, especially towards her dear, dear family . . . and also towards the new country that she was about to adopt, but—more importantly—that was about to adopt her. She loved the idea of finally being in America. She said that she thought Uncle Ferdinand and Aunt Alice looked well and relaxed, and she hoped that they not only looked well but also felt well, and were happy and content, and had already assimilated to their new home. Satisfied that this was indeed the case, dinner and conversation lasted long into the night. There was so much to catch up on; so much to tell; so much to ask. The entire conversation was in German, of course.

From the best of my observations, my mother was not shocked by her new surroundings. Always realistic and practical, she realized that—for the moment at least—there were no viable alternatives. Aside from that, she was happy and delighted to be reunited with closest and dearest family members in this manner. Somehow, as always, it would work.

Cousin Martha told my mother that she worked in a blouse factory located two or three blocks from her house. She told my mother that she had obtained a job for her at this same factory. Mother would start on Monday. Mother took the Amsterdam Avenue street car "uptown" for twenty blocks. The pay was based on piece work, thereby placing emphasis on speed, as well as ability. The pressure was on. Mother earned about $30 dollars for forty hours of work that first week, she recalls. After two weeks, Helen Thal, a cousin on the Lowenberg side, told my mother to "forget about that sweatshop job", for she had arranged a job for mother at her place of employment, also in the needle trade. Helen worked at a ladies' dress, suit and coat boutique on Madison Avenue by the name of "Rennele of Paris". Mr. Rennele was the designer and master tailor. His wife—a confident, well-dressed woman, as mother noted immediately—handled the "front of the store", namely the fussy ladies of Manhattan's Upper East Side. Mr. Rennele immediately struck mother as an especially decent, friendly, fair man. Mother worked for him for many, many years—eight to be exact—both on Madison Avenue, and later in Broadway's garment center. Her commute to Madison Avenue was, of course, somewhat longer. However, the pay, the working conditions and the entire milieu was far better, it was almost elegant. Starting at a grand $40 per week, she worked her way up from a "finisher" to a full-fledged dress maker, and later sample maker.

Back at Hamilton Place things did work out, sort of. The apartment, as we had originally observed, did not have a second bedroom. The living room had an "alcove", into which two narrow beds could fit lengthwise against the windows, sort of. A curtain provided some privacy, sort of. When Cousin Lore, now 23, was home for the weekend, she slept on the living room sofa. And yet, somehow, everybody had a great time. We were totally swept up in the intense happiness and great delight and the excitement of post-war America . . . its joy, its pace, its openness, its sense of security. Life in the America of 1946 was inexpensive. On Saturday mornings, Aunt Alice, my mother and I would go shopping at the nearby A& P. At the cost of a ten dollar bill, we could hardly carry home the food and the beverages and the other household products in the obligatory two-wheeler shopping cart and in our arms.

A certain routine settled in quickly. I started the age-appropriate sixth grade about a week after arriving in New York. Junior High School—P.S.115, located at 177th Street near Audubon Avenue, an excellent school serving the Washington Heights neighborhood, was a streetcar-ride away. The Haas apartment was outside its school district borders. I was, therefore, registered as living at Aunt Martha's home on 172nd Street. This "illegal maneuvering" frightened me. It made me feel insecure. It brought back memories of life in occupied Europe, living under the radar, attempting to blend in at any cost, constantly looking over one's shoulder. But once again there would be no alternative, I was told. I would have lunch at Aunt Martha's for three years—every weekday, except for holidays and vacation . . . and sometimes go to her house after school, only to walk home later when the coast was clear. In the morning, I would be careful not to be seen by teachers and pupils as I was getting off the streetcar. I would therefore go early. The same problem had to be negotiated every afternoon on the return trip. And it worked, sort of.

Because of the confines of the apartment on Hamilton Place, and perhaps because of the nature of the off-the-beaten-path neighborhood, Mother and I spent a lot of time at Aunt Martha's. As mentioned in an earlier chapter, Martha's family name was Schloss. She lived in a large third-flour apartment at the corner of 172nd Street and Broadway, with her husband Albert, and two sons, George and Gerry (formerly Gerhardt). The latter had served in the Army Air Corps during the war. This address was in the very heart of Washington Heights, the German-Jewish ghetto. From her corner apartment, one could glean the entire scene, especially on Saturday afternoons. Washington Heights, on the extreme west side of Manhattan and along the Hudson River, stretched from about 155th to the environs of the George Washington Bridge, covering Riverside Drive, Fort Washington Avenue, and Broadway. Ah, Broadway! On a sunny Saturday afternoon, one could stroll along Broadway, see everyone one knew, and hear nary a word of English. With the exception of A & P and perhaps a few other chain stores, this was still the era of the small, family owned and run specialty stores. You could go to the butcher, the baker, produce store, the cleaner, the haberdashery store, the barber and the beauty shop, etc., without having to speak a word of English. You quickly became friends with the shop owners, and you met all your friends and neighbors there. Washington Heights took on this unique flavor in the mid- to late Thirties, continued to blossom immediately after the war and remained that way for many, many years. Cousin Martha knew absolutely everyone in The Heights. A strong bond held this community together. Life was not easy for these immigrants. They found America in an unprecedented economic depression. Jobs were hard to find for these people who desperately needed work. Most were forced to take jobs below their educational qualifications and level of prior experience. The language barrier was a problem for most. After the harrowing experience of pre-war Germany, many found the work hard, harsh, demanding and stressful. Everybody in the family worked somewhere, somehow. Cousin Albert passed away prematurely, about a year after mother and I arrived in New York. The work and the stress and the past experiences in Nazi Germany were too much for his heart. It was just at the time that Martha was bringing her older maiden sister, Else, and her aged parents to America. Thankfully, they had survived the Holocaust in French camps. The third sibling, Edgar, an older brother and his family survived in Strasbourg. He was a French citizen, having moved to Strasbourg before the Nazi era. Both mother and I—separately—visited him and his wife, daughter and two sons, on several of our return trips to Europe. And later, in better times, mother and her second husband would meet them at the annual Haas Clan reunion in Switzerland. After Martha passed away, Else moved back to Strasbourg. Else was Mother's—and my—favorite cousin. She was highly intelligent, a talented pianist, witty and funny, open minded, in every sense a most generous person . . . and a great conversationalist. The hideous Nazi years—and her own sense of duty toward her rapidly aging parents—ruined a life filled with great potential. There were many ways to become a victim of the German nation, its people and its murderous leaders. Many, many lives were horribly and negatively changed, twisted, turned topsy-turvy, shortened and totally ruined . . . and left in the dust of ignorance, hate and bigotry. If we loved spending time at the Schloss apartment, Else made it even more enjoyable. Memories are only enhanced by such valuable souls.

However, she was not the only "star" on 172nd Street. Martha's older son, Jerry, ten years my senior, took me under his wing. His number one project: to teach me baseball. In the summer of 1947, he took me to my first baseball game, a night game: the Cleveland Indians vs. Yankees at Yankee Stadium. The 78,000-seat stadium was filled to capacity. Men still wore suits and hats to the stadium. The Indians were cruising to a 5-0 lead with Bob Feller pitching, when Tommy Henrich touched Feller for a two-run shot into the short right-field stands. In the bottom of the seventh inning Joe DiMaggio hit one of his patented monster-grand-slam home runs into the left field bleachers, giving the Yanks a 6-5 lead. Lou Boudreaux, the player-manager short stop of the Indians summoned the great Satchel Page in relief. Not only couldn't the Yankees hit the ball for the rest of the night, they couldn't see the ball for the rest of night. But it was too late—the Yankees won the game. However, Lou Boudreaux would take his team, including the first black American League player, to the World Series. It would only be the first of many trips to The Stadium with Jerry. I would be a Yankee fan many, many years . . . and a "Jerry-fan" to the present day. Such sweet memories enhanced my assimilation into American society and culture.

The fact was, all things considered, Mother and I settled in very well at the Haas home. Uncle Ferdinand and Aunt Alice were simply wonderful to us. Mother loved them both very much. There was never a disharmonious incident that I can recall. In the morning, the four—or sometimes five—of us took our turn in the one bathroom. Breakfast was as relaxed as possible or practical. The evening meals were a pleasure, with lots of opportunities for my mother and me to learn the ropes. Everybody enthusiastically reported their day's experiences. For my mother, America was weaving its charm.

*   *   *

As reported earlier, the London Lowenbergs had also planned to come to America after the war. They finally got their necessary "papers" and came to New York in 1947.

The new plan for my mother and me was not to impose on the Haas household any longer and move in with the three Lowenbergs. Alfred, my mother's much younger brother, was also scheduled to arrive in New York imminently and join us. Upon their arrival in New York, the Lowenbergs rented a large top-floor apartment at the corner of Riverside Drive and 160th Street. "Upper" Riverside Drive had once been a swank, elegant neighborhood . . . and it still wasn't what you could call "bad". It was safe and relatively clean. Apartment 7A, the corner apartment, looking out over Riverside Drive which, although somewhat diminished and faded from its former glory, nevertheless had a magnificent unobstructed view of the Hudson River, New Jersey's Palisade Heights and the George Washington Bridge. That—and its cool river breezes—would never diminish. The apartment had five bedrooms, including a maid's room beyond the kitchen, which was to be Cousin Fred's. There were two full bathrooms. The river-front dining room/living room combination was huge. There was even a furnishable foyer at the end of a long corridor. Aunt Dorothy and Uncle Sol moved into the master bedroom. Mother and I, at least for the time being, moved into the corner bedroom. One of the other bedrooms was intended for Alfred. The fifth, and last, bedroom was to be rented out to defray the rental cost of the apartment.

The Lowenbergs were able to "save" their *Lift*, the container that held all their furniture, household goods and some "valuables". Since so many refugees came to America without their lift and without any of their belongings, this was "a big deal" among the new immigrants, mother remembers. There was plenty of furniture to furnish the entire apartment. I think mother was more than a little envious. She and my father had so many beautiful things in their home, she would tell me. I could not remember. However, furniture and furnishings can be replaced, she would add, while human lives cannot be replaced. Anyway, Lift or no Lift, yet another communal living arrangement came into being. Did I like this any better than the last one? Did my mother? Not really. It may have made the school commute a little easier in that the school was now "only" sixteen city blocks away. However, I was nearly twelve. I wanted my own bedroom. This was not to be for a while. Almost at once, Mother and I missed Uncle Ferdinand and Aunt Alice.

But as usual, for my mother it was that familiar "stiff upper lip, it'll all work out" attitude. Yes, there was much more room; lots of air up on the seventh floor . . . and that priceless view; mother's commute to work was more-or-less the same. The neighborhood—in so-called "lower" Washington Heights—was an improvement. There was a cousin (on my father's side) by the name of Kahn—and her family—just two blocks away. Mother liked that. Nevertheless, Mother's satisfaction with this arrangement would be relatively short-lived. Yet, it lasted six long years.

*   *   *

My mother needed a social life, both within the extended family . . . and without. For that purpose her main resource was her old schoolmate, playmate and girl friend, Margot Beigel. Margot and her daughter, Astride, the latter about my age, had come to New York, via Paris, before the war. They lived in a rather elegant apartment—door man and all—at the corner of West End Avenue and 73rd Street, at the center of the "real" upper West

Side. Margot's story was oddly strange and profoundly sad. She had married an affluent French Jew named Beigel and moved to Paris. When conditions for Jews in Germany deteriorated more and more, Margot brought her aging mother and her younger sister to Paris. When it became clear that life for Jews would be equally untenable in France, all four emigrated to America and set up household in New York. It was during this time that the Frenchman fell in love with the younger sister. He divorced his wife, Margot, and married the younger sister. He "bankrolled" the apartment on West End Avenue and sent Astride to a private day school near the Museum of Natural History off Central Park West. The elderly mother-in-law lived with the Frenchman and his new bride, and would forever be the go-between in this sad—and at times dramatic—triangle. Margot, an attractive, smart, worldly woman worked as a legal secretary in a posh office of attorneys. By the time my mother and I came to New York, Margot's new life style had taken on a life of its own. She had a large circle of friends with a couple of cousins thrown in. She entertained a lot. For mother it was an atmosphere quite different from that on Hamilton Place and later at Riverside Drive. The parties were gay and the company was good, as was the food and drink. Mother knew a few of "Margot's people" from Mannheim days. As for the others, she blended in easily and made new friends. I would usually go with her since I had a built-in playmate in Astride. We'd wander off to her room and play games, talk and listen to records, only to surface for the always excellent food and refreshments. However, I think most of all, Mother and I enjoyed the leisurely weekend afternoons with Margot and Astride. We would walk over to 72nd Street, a lively area, and have coffee and cake at Café Éclair's . . . or perhaps at La Cupole across the street. The West 72nd Street neighborhood was a sort of an upscale Washington Heights, again infused with many, many immigrants, mostly of the pre-war variety of Western European Jews, for here you also found Jews from Vienna, Prague and Budapest, who were able to bring their money with them, or had already prospered in the short years in America. They all came to Café Éclair's and La Cupole, and it was "party time" all over. In this setting, and for years to come, Margot was extremely generous and kind to my mother. It was just what the doctor ordered, as they say. Mother's "uptown" social life would be quite different. Adding the many Lowenberg uncles and cousins to the Haas Clan, plus old friends and some new ones, there always seemed to be a large crowd as well. Mother enjoyed the company of the Wolfs on nearby 164th Street and the Goldseckers in our apartment building. However, these people could not afford the theater or the opera or concerts at Carnegie Hall. Nor could they afford to eat out in style . . . and of course neither could my mother. Therefore, social activities centered around home entertainment. Canasta games were the fad of the day . . . or just sitting around *schmoozing* . . . whatever . . . but, always with coffee and cake. Mother and I remember the first time we watched television (later, in 1947). A cousin of my father, Agathe, who lived in Jackson Heights, Queens, with her husband and son, invited us to their house on a Sunday evening to watch the Ed Sullivan Show. About a dozen chairs were placed facing the TV, and everybody was greatly excited about watching mostly "snow" on the tiniest of Dumont sets equipped with a kind of magnifying gadget/attachment. Naturally, after Ed, coffee and cake was served.

Speaking of the early days of television, I fondly recall Alfred taking me to the local ice cream parlor to see the Milton Berle Show. New York had these wonderful ice cream parlors all over town. The quarter (25 cents) Sunday was topped with real, old fashioned whipped cream. The bars were not the only ones to have TVs at that fledgling stage of the medium.

In the meantime, life with the Lowenbergs at Riverside Drive went on. Mother felt secure at work, and as per pre-arrangement, was able to contribute to the expenses of the combined household. Mother seemed to remember a weekly sum of about six dollars for room and board, so to speak. The rented room brought in about the same amount for the Lowenbergs. Sometimes, I would meet Mother and/or Aunt Dora in the evening after work at the 157th Street I.R.T. subway station and help with the food shopping. The small immigrant-owned super market on the corner of 158th Street carried everything, and the language *du jour* was, of course, German.

Having that first winter in New York behind us, the spring of 1947 brought on new challenges for my mother. She would have to plan for my Bar Mitzvah in December of that year. There was also the polio problem. Before the oral medication and the vaccine were invented, New Yorkers worried a great deal about their children's exposure to polio. The relatively affluent sent their children to summer camps. Other such families rented summer-long cottages or hotel rooms in the Catskills or beyond. Those who could not afford that, did nothing and hoped and prayed.

The Lowenbergs had a different idea. They had a very dear first cousin living in Greensboro, North Carolina, married to one Arthur Goodman, a young American-born Jew. Still childless, their business had prospered sufficiently to enable them to buy a modest, but nice house in one of the early suburban areas of town. It was suggested, and they very kindly agreed, that I would spend the summer with them. Since I was able to negotiate the Swiss railway system, everyone thought, I would surely survive a direct, overnight sleeper-car journey to Greensboro. And I did. In case you wonder, dear reader, where the money came from to finance such trips around the land, naturally, it came from the Neuburgers. I recall having such a wonderful summer with the Goodmans that it was repeated in the summer of 1948. However, upon my arrival at the Greensboro train station in 1947, I received quite a culture shock. There was a waiting room, rest rooms, water fountains with signs reading "Coloreds Only". Were these signs the equivalent of Nazi-German's "No Jews Allowed"? Hell yeah they were, and I was about to witness life in The South for the first time. Racism, based on color, was totally new to me . . . and it was shocking. My very first contact with black Americans was in Switzerland immediately after the war. As the Armed Forces rotated their personnel out of the battle zones of Germany—many to reunite with their families for the first time in several years—some of these troop trains would stop in St. Gallen. We boys would go down to the train station and barter with the troops for their insignia. An officer's insignia was of special collecting value and prestige. We offered chocolate, picture post cards and other small, inexpensive souvenirs. It was on these troop trains that I saw my first black man. This "train fad" soon passed, and any encounter with black people was equally soon forgotten, without any trace of afterthoughts and/or questions. The fact that there were black faces in this world made absolutely no impact on me. At age ten, Racism was not a word in my lexicon. Later, in New York, living near black people, being with them in subway trains, on the streets, in the shops, was simply no problem for me at that time of my youth. Racism based on color was a non-issue with me. Unfortunately, sadly, I was just being naïve. Why did I have to go to a school in another school district? Why were there no black boys and girls in my school? Why was the term "shwartze" taboo and never to be used with black people within hearing range? My introduction to American racism, not just southern racism, would come later in life.

However, back to the summer of 1947. I immediately liked the Goodmans and the Goodman's house. I had my own room. On those really hot southern nights (before air conditioning), I would sleep on the large screened-in porch. There was plenty of privacy, as the Goodmans lived at the edge of a forest . . . a little creepy perhaps, but I had survived a lot worse. We would have dinner alfresco, and I learned how to eat watermelon in great quantities and drink immense amounts of iced tea in huge glasses. During the day, the Goodmans had arranged playmates for me amongst their neighbors and friends. We would usually go swimming to beat the heat.

On other days, I would go to the business with Arthur. He was a wholesaler of just about all items usually carried by gas station convenience stores. His customers would largely come to his place of business to make their purchases. However, to augment income, he would fill up his station wagon with his wares and travel the rural roads of North Carolina . . . and I would accompany him. What great days those turned out to be. What wonderful "characters" I would meet. They all knew—and rather liked—Arthur. And he indeed sported a casual, friendly, honest non-threatening persona. They forgave him for being Jewish . . . and in time that hardly was a factor. I liked these people of the rural South. They were easy-going. Life moved a good bit slower than up North. Yet, they seemed hardworking and honest as well. They socialized easily and never seemed to be alone in their convenience stores alongside their gas stations. These were the days before self-service. They'd fill up the gas tank, check the oil under your hood and wash the windshield. They made the time to chat a while. I also liked their music. After a while, we'd say a cordial goodbye and "move on down the road a ways" to the next customer. It was hot. Once in a great while, we'd see a dead snake on the side of the road, of which many were still dirt roads. Or, we'd see some barefoot boys, white and black, saunter down the road on their way to the nearest swimming hole. The children managed to play together. It was the adults who could not live together. Ignorance and hate and false traditions keeps them apart to this very day.

One day, we took a pretty long car trip over to Fayetteville to visit the other cousins, the Greens (formerly Gruenebaum). John Green, who had come to America before the war, served with the U.S. Army in Europe. Starting with a G.I. loan and an army buddy partner, he was to become quite affluent, a true example of that famous "only in America" phrase. Later, the Greens were to be extremely kind to Aunt Dora for the rest of her days. I saw them once again during my six-week R.O.T.C. summer camp training at Ft. Bragg in the summer of 1955.

Upon my return to New York, Bar Mitzvah training continued and intensified. Mother had joined a small congregation near our apartment just east of Broadway on 158th Street. Congregation Tikwoh Chadoscho was composed entirely of German-Jewish immigrants and refugees. Its spiritual leader, a Rabbi Schottland, was the former rabbi/cantor of my late father's hometown synagogue in Ruelzheim, Germany. Schottland was also my Hebrew teacher. The big news was that Aunt Selma and her older son, Walter, were coming to attend my Bar Mitzvah. They stayed in New York, in separate hotels, for a little over a week during that record setting cold and snowy winter of 1947-1948. The snow drifts at Riverside Drive were waist high. However, as no one could afford a car, we managed quite well. After all, the subways always ran. Mother planned a very nice family luncheon in the large dining room/living room. As "host", Uncle Sally (Sol), along with Uncle Ferdinand, re-established as the patriarch of the Haas Clan, "officiated". There would be no catering service. Aunt Dora and my mother did all the cooking and set a beautiful table with the fine table linens and the "good silver" from the Lowenberg lift. A reception followed from three—to six o'clock. Considering our modest means, it was a great and memorable day for me. I believe it was a wonderful day for all the relatives. Mother had pulled it off once again, and the presence of the Neuburgers made it unforgettable. It also put an exclamation point on their earlier pronouncement that they would do everything within their power to keep up the special relationship. They once again spoiled mother and me with money and gifts. Walter was especially wonderful to my mother and me. Everyone in our extended family loved him. Due to his ongoing military duties, he had to return to Switzerland separately and sooner than his mother. No one could have guessed that he would not be with us for much longer.

As reported earlier, my mother kept everything. And so, a two-sided note from Aunt Selma survived, written on a personalized stationery card. I will translate. The card read: 'Dear Ernstl (not a typo)! At this time of your Bar Mitzvah, I bring you my most sincerely good wishes. May you have a wonderful future. It is also in the memory of dear Uncle David, who—as you know—was very close to you that I spend these days with you, my dear young man . . . and with your mother . . . and with all your nearest and dearest loved ones. I hope that you will always look back on this day, the day on which you were so specially honored, with great pride and joy. I now give you my very best wishes directly from my heart. Your Aunt Selma.' The note was accompanied by a generous U.S. Savings Bond.

*   *   *

On November 15, 1948, Uncle Sol passed away. He was a religiously observant man, and to my mother and me a very kind man. He would be sorely missed. He was 62. The murderous Nazi years of the Thirties, the harsh and tenuous life in London and the menial work in New York were too much for his already-weakened heart. He went to sleep in his bed and never woke up. Holocaust victims surface in countless variations.

*   *   *

In the summer of 1949, my mother no longer needed to send me to North Carolina. She negotiated a leave of absence with her employer, Mr. Rennele. She took a summer job at a small hotel in Hunter in the northern portion of the Catskill Mountains. I was able to stay with her for the entire summer. The hotel was owned by the Lustig family, friends of my mother and father in Mannheim. They had come to New York before the war with just enough money to buy a row house and a small luncheonette in the Astoria section of Queens, New York. The hotel purchase followed in early 1948. The clientele was strictly of the Washington Heights variety. Some families booked by the week, some stayed the entire summer, with the fathers coming up for the weekend. The Lustigs had two daughters, one a year older, the other about three years older than I was. They made wonderful playmates and "senior advisors", especially now that I was becoming aware of the opposite sex. Mother and I are still in contact with "the girls". They are now grandparents, of course. Mother doubled as a chamber maid and a waitress . . . and she loved it. It was, in fact, a great summer for my mother and me. Many years later, when both my mother and Erna Lustig were widowed, they would travel together to the family reunion in summer and to Florida in winter.

However, halfway through the summer, we received devastatingly shocking news: Walter Neuburger had passed away after a short, hopeless bout with stomach cancer. He was twenty-seven years old.

CHAPTER 16

America—Part II

1950 and Beyond

In early 1950, most likely because of the tragic and untimely death of her son, Walter, during the past year, Aunt Selma got in touch with my mother for a special "request". Aunt Selma wrote that she—and Hanns—would like Ernest to come back to Switzerland for a visit over the summer vacation. They would pay for all expenses and send the tickets, of course. And perhaps, Ernest could see his grandmother and Aunt Regina once again. Aunt Selma wrote that she just wanted a young voice around the house, one that would remind her—most pleasantly and warmly—of the wonderful days when Uncle David and Walter graced the house. She needed "something", she wrote. I had just passed my fifteenth birthday. In theory my mother agreed. But, she asked Uncle Ferdinand for advice, which was affirmative. However, my mother held out one disclaimer: Ernest would not be permitted to fly. He would have to make the solo passage by ship. Civilians and non-big-business types flying across the Atlantic remained somewhat of a rarity. To complicate matters, just days before my scheduled departure, the Korean War broke out. Would this be the beginning of the Third World War? Was it a great risk in letting Ernest travel to Europe? Mother decided to ask for Uncle Ferdinand's advice once again. "No", he said, "no risk, nor danger at all. This is just a small war that no one cares about in a country far away It will be over in a couple of weeks. As a matter of fact, I just shipped some bulk merchandise to Denmark and Germany", he added. And that sealed the bargain.

In actuality, my mother's thinking was just the slightest bit "fuzzy". Flying would simply have meant someone dropping me off at the Swissair's New

York ticket counter and someone picking me up at Swissair arrival terminal at Zurich's Kloten Airport. This was pointed out to Kate. However, her decision prevailed, thus calling for a convoluted and detailed set of plans, especially as Switzerland is not near an ocean. I would sail—tourist class—to Genoa on the Italian Line's *Conte Biancamano*. I thought the sea voyage was exhilarating, exciting and adventurous. My adult shipmates—strangers all—talked to me and marveled over such a young boy traveling alone. As 1950 was Holy Year in Italy, they all asked whether I was going to visit the Pope. Negative folks, sorry! The deck's purser, and the people assigned to my dining room table, were kind enough to keep an eye on me. We had about two rough days and nights at sea. And, I did throw up on the stairs between decks. But, once again, I survived to tell the story. Let me add, at this point, that during the Holocaust years, the vast majority of the Italian people were very kind to their Jews. And, everyone knows of the fate that awaited their Fascist wartime leader.

At the Genoa pier I would be met by my mother's first cousin, Alice, and her son, Peter, and the three of us would take a train to Milan. Alice had survived the war in Milan. She and her former husband, a physician—both from Mannheim—had emigrated to Milan before the war. By this time she was divorced. Alice was my mother's playmate and great friend in Mannheim. Mother spoke of her often. I stayed with Alice for a few days. Her apartment was small, seemed somewhat impoverished, and lacked modern appliances and conveniences, such as a refrigerator, considering Milan's hot summer climate. However, things of that nature don't really matter for a fifteen-year-old adventurer. All meals were eaten at home. Alice was a great cook, utilizing all those fresh Italian fruits and vegetables, and all those other wonderful Italian ingredients. Peter, a couple of years younger than me, was a good playmate and guide, always under Alice's watchful eye of course. I loved Milan and the Italian atmosphere. The Italian people seemed friendly, warm and laid-back. But, most of all I loved Cousin Alice. She was attractive, a brilliant pianist with a huge sense of humor and an equally huge heart. Unbeknownst to me at the time, of course, I would have the good fortune to see Alice again soon. For now, parting time came only too soon. Alice, with Peter in tow, put me on an international express train to Zurich, where Aunt Selma and Hanns picked me up on the platform.

We drove back to St. Gallen. On the surface neither Number 40, nor the town, had changed at all. But that would be a most misleading observation. So far, Hanns, still single, was subdued . . . and Aunt Selma almost constantly in tears. Her sorrow was sadly and understandably beyond all bounds. She was brave enough and loving enough to say that some of her tears were indeed tears of joy to see me, hold me and have me around the house once again. I was in tears as well and commiserated with her grief. That is, as well as a fifteen-year-old can handle such dark situations. Aunt Selma, now sixty-six years of age, seemed to have aged a great deal since her visit to New York in January of 1948. The one-year mourning period was not yet over. The next day, we visited Walter's grave and, of course, Uncle David's grave: My two dear friends . . . gone. I had to weep again. As I write this paragraph, now exactly sixty years later, I weep once more. Walter had so much potential, so much to give. The house seemed somehow empty now; there was a large, pervasive void. It would be a long summer.

Despite the grief and the lingering cloud of death, I quickly readjusted to the routine of the Neuburger household. Luxury was back in style, at least for six weeks. All my friends were right there where I had left them, including Heinz and Marion et al., available for play, or perhaps a swim in nearby Lake Constance (*Bodensee*) on sunny, mild days and a movie on the cool, rainy days. However, most of all, I loved being back on the Neuburger business premises. I loved spending time in the office and the factory. All those old "friends" were there too. Aunt Selma would come around at the afternoon break and bring wonderful snacks for the executive staff: an excellent cake, or perhaps the freshest, best buttered soft pretzels I ever ate. In general, Aunt Selma seemed to spend more time at the office now. Handing out the weekly pay envelopes, for example, was a signal to the staff that she would remain involved. It was a good diversion for her. As for the business and my future, the tiny seeds that had been sown when I was eight or nine or ten years old began to produce their first modest sprouts.

The big surprise treat for me came about halfway through the summer. We were going to Florence, Italy. We left in two cars and with a lot of baggage, the other car being driven by Willy Brown, a jovial, older bachelor cousin of the Neuburgers, employed in the business as a salesman, and a very close friend of the family. We crossed the Alps over the spectacular San Bernardino mountain pass . . . yes, where the dogs come from . . . highest road elevation 6778 feet. (This was before all the tunnels.) In mid-summer we started a snowball fight. We soon descended and, via Lugano, arrived in Milan, where we spent the night at the well-known and elegant Principe-Savoya Hotel. (I would return there on business trips in the Sixties and Seventies.) Then, on to the magnificence that is Florence. The full glory and cultural impact of Florence is perhaps wasted on a fifteen-year-old . . . the beauty of the city and its breathtaking surroundings: the hills, the sun, the warmth, trips into the hillside for leisurely lunches or dinners and the soft evening air that followed the heat of the day. And then there's all that art, a bounty of the masters almost beyond belief. We spent a lovely week there, at ease . . . and reunited. There would be no rush; no one-two-three off the bus and back on the bus; no twenty countries in twenty-one days routine.

At the end of the week, Willy drove Aunt Selma back to St. Gallen. Hanns and I went on to Nice. From Florence, Hanns and I drove westward toward the Mediterranean, passing Pisa on our right. We drove northward along the sea and spent the night in the vicinity of Rapallo. Then, we drove on to Nice. Hanns dropped me off at the Maison de Vieillards La Colline in the Quartier Saint-Antoine, Nice, and picked me up a few days later. He was always so kind to my grandmother and Aunt Regina. In the meantime, he stayed at the Carlton in Cannes for a little bachelor vacation, for which—I would learn considerably later—the Riviera is tailor-made. I was exceedingly glad that I was once again able to visit my grandmother and Aunt Regina. They seemed very much unchanged, content, bright, in relatively good health, and well taken care of. Of course, they wanted to hear all about America, now that a major portion of the Haas Clan was reunited there. Most of all, they wanted to know how my mother was doing. I told them that she acclimated very well and loved America and New York; that she remained very, very fond of Uncle Ferdinand and Aunt Alice; and that she generally felt secure in the safety net of the cousins and second cousins. I told them that I enjoyed school, was doing well in school, and had lots of new friends. As for La Colline and the surrounding area, I was again dazzled by the beauty of the Riviera. However, parting with the two wonderful ladies was difficult, as I had no idea when—and if—I would see them again. And, at summer's end, returning to Riverside Drive was a "mixed bag".

1952 was my mother's year. On March 31st, she was naturalized as a citizen of the United States by the U.S. District Court for the Southern District of New York at New York! It was her happiest day in nearly twenty years. Need I say more? In the summer of 1952, my mother made her first trip back to Europe. She would no longer be forced to travel with the "papers" of a stateless person. She now carried a passport respected by the entire world. She was a whole person once again. Aunt Selma had invited my mother to Hanns' wedding, all expenses paid. Utilizing her vacation at work, my mother was only away for two weeks. Most importantly, it now enabled my mother to travel to Nice to see her mother and aunt for one more joyous visit. That was indeed fortunate. It also clearly illustrated how much we were still dependent on the Neuburgers, and how very willing they were to extend their courtesies to other members of our family, while freely and graciously continuing their genuine love and generosity to my mother and me. My mother gratefully accepted their kindness, but was very happy to return to New York with a bagful of pictures and stories and memories.

The following year, 1953, the Neuburgers wanted me back in Switzerland . . . all expenses paid, of course. I was only too happy to go . . . this time by airplane. By this time, I was a student at City College of New York (CCNY). Mother suggested that a "certain gentleman" would drive us to the airport. It was my mother's boyfriend and suitor. Now and then, here and there during the past weeks, I had casually heard of him, but had never met him. His name was Edmond Hecht, a tall, slightly portly gentleman of good bearing, about fifty years old. He drove a light blue Plymouth . . . and that was about all I knew about him.

In the early—and mid-Fifties—Europe was very wary of the Russians relatively close to its borders. It was the widespread belief in Western Europe that the Russians had plans to attack and conquer Western Europe . . . at least to march to the Rhein at first. The Swiss felt threatened as well. They believed that Russia would not respect Switzerland's historic state of neutrality. Also, the Swiss felt that the Russians did not particularly like them. Hanns, considering this scenario, was not about to make the same mistake the financially comfortable German Jews made twenty years earlier. To establish a possible "go to" destination, he purchased a ramie plantation in Brazil. His old school chum accepted the position to manage the plantation. He relocated his family—his wife and two young children—to a large jungle clearing, the site of the plantation. Once the deal was done, and the plantation fully operational again under the new management, Hanns began to visit Brazil at least once a year. He would always schedule his trip via New York in order to visit my mother and me. And, we were always delighted to see him. Just as an example, it was he who convinced me to enter the R.O.T.C. program at CCNY . . . and darn good advice it was. The war was still raging in Korea. It was important for me to remain in college even if the war intensified. "And besides", Hanns said, "it is always better to be an officer".

My 1953 trip was especially enjoyable and very much remains in my fondest memories. I found Aunt Selma in far better spirits. Hanns, now married, had regained his cheerfulness. He married Vera Teitler, the "girl down the street". She was young, ten years younger than Hanns, and gorgeous. The first child, Jacqueline, had arrived earlier that May. Vera's brother, and only sibling, was an old cub-scout buddy. It was wonderful to see everyone again. Vera's parents greeted me warmly, and I remained friendly with them throughout their lives, especially with Sam, Vera's father.

This trip again gave me the happy opportunity to see grandmother and Aunt Regina. Again, we had a wonderful time together . . . the generations inter-acting so easily and lovingly. Both ladies facilitated that through their optimism, humor and easy-going style. All the conversation was once again about America, about the entire extended family, about college, but also about the Neuburgers. However, sadly, this would be the last time that I would see the ladies. They both passed away in 1954. Appropriately, they share a joint grave, high above the Cote d'Azure.

Shortly after my return to St. Gallen, tanned and content, I received an interesting telephone call from my mother. She said that she intended to marry Edmond Hecht. She asked whether or not, she and Edmond should wait with the marriage proceedings until I returned to New York in early September. I answered somewhat curtly: "If you have to ask, just proceed whenever you want to". After all "he" was a perfect stranger and was about to steal my own dear mother away from me. In Freudian parlance this was all very normal. They waited!

I concluded my lovely stay in St. Gallen. This time, I had something special to return to.

Edmond was born in Belgium, studied in Lausanne, Switzerland, but lived most of his life in Paris and Frankfurt. After fleeing to neutral Portugal, he managed to reach America's shores just prior to its entry into World War Two. He was able to take a tidy sum of money with him. He rented an apartment in Rego Park, New York, and went to his stock broker's office every day, where he mainly sat and watched the ticker tape. When he proposed to my mother, he rented a larger, two-bedroom apartment nearby. My mother quit her job and was only too happy to say good-bye to Aunt Dora, Cousin Fred, and 870 Riverside Drive, Apartment 7A. Soon after my return and shortly after my mother's forty-fifth birthday, on September 23, 1953, on the fourteenth day of Tishri of the Judaic year of 5714, Mother did indeed get married. The aforementioned Rabbi Schottland performed a short ceremony at 7A. A reception for the nearest and dearest followed, with coffee and cake of course. That night my mother and Edmond moved into the new apartment at 66-15 Wetherole Street, Forest Hills, New York. I remained at Riverside Drive for a few more days (and nights), while the happy couple enjoyed their honeymoon in Washington, visiting Alfred in Baltimore on the way back. At that time, I joined them at the Forest Hills apartment.

This would be the first time since the beginning of the war that my mother would have her own home, her own kitchen, and everything that came with it . . . especially privacy and the right to peace and quiet. She had lived the communal life since 1942. After eleven years, independence meant a great deal to my mother. I believe that the prospect of this new, emancipated life figured strongly in my mother's decision to remarry generally, and to marry Edmond in particular. Wetherole Street—and that time all of Forest Hills and Rego Park—was a lovely residential area. It was clean and safe, and the apartment building was well-kept. At the time we moved in it had a door man, that New York city dweller's "seal of approval" for real—or more likely faux—elegance. It also had a much coveted parking garage for Edmond's Plymouth. It was the only apartment building in the immediate surrounding area of neat townhouses. It was a predominantly Jewish neighborhood, convenient to the IND Subway and the Long Island Railroad stations. In a way, the "honeymoon" continued.

To be rather blunt about it, at first, I did not particularly like Edmond. And, for my mother, reality would set in soon enough. Edmond's financial assets may have been sufficient for a small bachelor apartment and a simple life in New York. However, the larger apartment and two additional mouths to feed was quite another matter. Edmond suggested that my mother go back to work. She refused. Why should she go to work while he sat on his derriere watching the stock market tape pass by. And, he wasn't even a very good investor! I guess the honeymoon was over. Mother suggested that Edmond find a job post-haste, which he accomplished—much to his credit—very quickly. Then and only then, mother opened her own dressmaker's "shop" in the apartment, and through word-of-mouth, almost immediately became very busy. This working arrangement would continue for almost thirty years. Her remarkable inner strengths, her problem-solving ability, and all the positive aptitudes I've mentioned in the length and breadth of this book once again served to overcome crisis. And, mother was content with this work. Her "clients" soon became her friends. She had more work than she could handle. Working at home suited her, and she did not want to expand.

In retrospect, I was also happy to leave Riverside Drive. Living there had become a strain on mother. Cousin Fred, fourteen years older than me, had tried at times to be a "big brother" to me. He would take me to his social club's soccer matches and to the occasional movie. But, he was no Jerry Schloss. Fred and I never really clicked. Under our new living arrangement in Queens, I had a rather long subway commute to CCNY. But, in the New York metropolitan area that's normal. A good friend from

High School and the early years of college now lived nearby. And, I kept all my Washington Heights friends. Just as I had loved junior and senior high School, I loved CCNY from the very beginning. It was liberating and elevating. And, it was free. Riding on the E or F Train, changing to the A Train at the Seventh Avenue station, in my Senior R.O.T.C. uniform several times a week seemed pretty spiffy to me. My studies continued to go well, and I graduated with the Class of June 1955. Due to a technicality, I was to attend R.O.T.C. summer camp after graduation. I spent six sweaty weeks at Fort Bragg, North Carolina, and was duly commissioned there on August 5th. Out of the 1600 cadets, there were about ten of us in this same—and somewhat unusual—situation. The Commanding General of the Third Army, one Lt. Gen. Hickey, handed me my reserve commission with the words "from the President of the United States". It was—and still is—the proudest moment of my life. In the short time span of nine years, I had completely assimilated to American life. I flew back to New York (via Raleigh) immediately after the ceremony and the parade in our honor . . . in uniform, shiny new gold bars on my shoulders, standing about as tall as I ever stood in life. "Only in America!", I thought to myself. I wonder if anyone noticed that smile across my face.

However, my orders called for starting active duty in November 1955. That left quite a time gap. And, how does one fill such a gap? Hanns and Aunt Selma to the rescue once again. The trip materialized because we all believed that I would eventually be ordered to Korea. A ceasefire agreement had been reached there, but frequent troop rotation still required many officers and enlisted personnel to be sent to the frozen peninsula. It remained an unpleasant place. The danger of new hostilities breaking out again existed then and still exists today.

A trip to Switzerland would be a perfect opportunity to discuss post-service plans in greater detail. Leaving in late August, I spent the Jewish High Holidays in St. Gallen. I attended synagogue and proudly stood next to Hanns. He still had the two seats with the prayer books and shawls kept in the little cabinet in front of each seat. Nothing had changed whatsoever. The Teitler men, father and son, stood nearby. Marion's father stood across the sanctuary in his lifelong place. Rabbi Rothschild, a modern man and an excellent speaker, was still at the helm. And many old familiar friends' faces were scattered throughout the still vital congregation. Oh, the women sat upstairs. In this typical, European "liberal" setting, with organ and choir, it was, however, customary for the women to sit in the balcony . . . and customs don't fall easily . . . and haven't to this day. This comfortable, easy familiarity with the people and the surroundings engulfed me all too readily. After services, the Neuburger family—including me—formed the accustomed "reception line", and everyone (!) walked through the line. That was tradition too. Warm holiday greetings—and the occasional kiss—were exchanged. That's how things worked in St. Gallen. That was the pecking order in action.

Time passed quickly. Just before my return to America, Hanns asked me an interesting question: "Do you know how to drive a car?" When I replied in the negative, he wanted to know why. "In New York City one doesn't need a car. Besides, I get one scratch on Edmond's beloved Plymouth, I'd never hear the end of it," I replied. "Well," Hanns replied, "don't you think it would be helpful to know how to drive a car in the American army? What if they want you to drive a Jeep? You know, that's what lieutenants do. Upon your return to New York, I want to take driving lessons immediately. You don't have much time before reporting for duty. I'll pay for the lessons." I quickly agreed. Being just a few months short of my twenty-first birthday, I thought perhaps this is not such a bad idea. The day after I arrived in New York, I called a nearby driving school. The next day I was behind the wheel. I took five lessons, took the driving test the following day and passed.

A few days later I packed my bag and traveled to Fort Benning, North Carolina. I checked in at the Infantry School for eighteen weeks of very necessary—and excellent—training before receiving our specific troop assignments. It was November 14, 1955, six weeks before my twenty-first birthday. I won't bore the reader with all the details, except to mention that for six weeks I couldn't buy an alcoholic drink anywhere in the State of Georgia, except at the Officer's Club. As far the Army Infantry School was concerned, we were officers and they treated us as such: no surprises, no harassment, no B.S. The new lieutenants bonded quickly, and several lasting friendships were formed. A young lieutenant in my platoon, a recent graduate of Niagara University, Bill Crerend and I quickly became friends at Ft. Benning. At the time of this writing, the friendship between us—and our families—remains better than ever.

However, my previous trepidations about Korea were correct. I didn't really think that the fact that my records clearly stated that I was a German language expert would change anything. Absolutely no one reads those records. Everyone agreed that Korea would most likely be our destination after graduating from the Basic Infantry Officers Course. Imagine then, how surprised—and pleased—all 176 of us were when the orders came down: half the class assigned to Germany, the other half to Hawaii . . . in alphabetical order. We all received some leave time and a final reporting date for overseas duty. Living in the First Army district, I was to leave from McGuire Air Force Base, adjacent to Fort Dix. Quite buoyantly, I returned to New York and decided not to linger. My relationship with my stepfather, Edmund, was still . . . shaky, to say it as diplomatically as I can. Wetherole Street was by no means my favorite place. After a week or so, *Wanderlust* set in, and I reported to McGuire A.F.B. I was assigned to the 86th Infantry Regiment of the 10th Division stationed in Schweinfurt, Germany. At this point, I could have spoken to the personnel officer and pointed out my German language skills, and how they might benefit the U.S.Army. I decided against that option for two reasons. First, I wanted to do what I was trained for. Second, I didn't want to be assigned to some army intelligence school and then to some covert intelligence unit and spend the next two years under cover in East Germany. (I later met people doing exactly that.) So, before I knew it, I was the leader of the second platoon, A Company. My company commander, Captain Gene Marder, was a Jewish West Point graduate, Class of 1950, wounded in Korea, a great guy, who remained a life-long friend to me. I still maintain regular contact with Gene's widow, Margaret. As coincidence would have it, the aforementioned General Hickey's son was also a company commander in the First Battalion. A classmate and best friend of Captain Marder, he too was a gentleman's gentleman with whom I am also in contact to the present day. The aforementioned 2nd Lt. Crerend showed up in Schweinfurt a few days after me and was assigned to Capt. Hickey's company.

However, as soon as it "slipped out" that I speak, read and write German perfectly, I was transferred to Regimental Headquarters to be the German-American relations officer, "slotted" in the Table of Organization as Regimental Assistant Adjutant, a job normally assigned to a substantially senior officer. So, picture this: A twenty-one year-old Jewish "kid" from New York City born in Germany, who in fact hated the Germans, having to interact with them on a daily basis. Among my many assignments outside the regiment, I acted as the "senior" liaison officer to the New German Army who was participating in their first N.A.T.O. field exercise. I operated under the auspices of U.S. Fifth Corps. The reason for all this was that there simply were no German-speaking officers in Germany. There were, of course, recently-drafted German-speaking enlisted men. However, they could not be authorized for the duties I performed, many of which were financial in nature. For example: One of our tanks, making a careless turn in a small nearby village, took a big chunk out of Herr Fritz's house . . . or a bunch of drunken G.I.'s wrecked Herr Adolph's bar on a Saturday night . . . or a German father with his highly pregnant wedding-dress-clad daughter in tow storming into the Adjutant's office, insisting to see the commanding officer, in an effort to find the father of the yet-unborn child, etc., etc . . . 24/7/365. As much as I disliked the Germans (I told them that I was Swiss.), I must say that the job had its moments and its many "perks." Rubbing elbows with the Major General who commanded the division became routine. If I mentioned all my experiences this book would be a lot longer. So I'll desist, except for the wild-boar night-time hunt; the "strange" trip to Berlin, including East Berlin; the baseball bat shortage crisis—Bill was player/manager of our regimental baseball team, in addition to his regular duties—and its immediate Colonel-ordered helicopter purchasing junket to the PX in Frankfurt; the Major—my boss—and the Carman-Gia shopping days; the German caddies on the golf course calling me—among other things—a "duffer" behind my back, not suspecting that I understood their every word; likewise the gruesome tale of the officer's club German-speaking waitress who made disparaging remarks about us Americans after we complained about the price of the strawberries, you know—important matters like these and in effect your tax dollars at work.

The time passed quickly. However, most importantly, among my fellow officers and colleagues, most of them R.O.T.C.-bred, many life-long friendships were born that last to this very day. Fifteen years after our discharge, we had our first reunion. Fifteen couples, with children, attended. Of the fifteen, I was the only Jew. (Later another Jewish couple, from Iowa, started to attend.) We continued our reunions on a biannual basis. Although our attendance is down somewhat, due to death or physical impairment, the reunions are still great fun, and the core is holding for now. Of course my good friend Bill Crerend and his beautiful wife, Dolores, attend these reunions. He hasn't missed one yet. Bill and I exchange e-mail almost every day and speak on the phone once a week. He lives in Westchester County, New York. We couldn't have been more "opposite" in makeup. Bill is of Irish-Catholic descent—a tall, good-looking jock, who attended college on a basketball/baseball scholarship. I am none of these . . . not even close. Permit me to add that several other close friendships developed—and are still maintained: among them my "room mate" in Schweinfurt (We turned two rooms and shared bath into a little bachelor apartment.) . . . and a young lieutenant who was a superb career officer and attained the lofty rank of Major General.

However, the greatest "plus" of this assignment was in fact its proximity to Switzerland. I could now continue my relationship with Aunt Selma and Hanns almost at will by simply crossing one border. Thanks to my "only slightly and lovingly used" 1955 two-tone Chevy—fins and all—that I bought from Sgt. Reynolds in D Company, I made the trip as frequently as possible. On one of these furloughs, Hanns and Vera and I vacationed once again on the Riviera at the Old Beach Hotel in Monte Carlo. However, far more importantly, Hanns and I spent time aplenty to fine-tune the plan for my return to St. Gallen on a permanent basis and enter the Neuburger firm. Hanns was absolutely serious about this. He needed a Number Two, especially during his absences from the business. For me it was a childhood dream come true. For Aunt Selma, who was slowly and carefully briefed, it was primarily "what Uncle David would have wanted," as she put it. The plan was that after discharge from the military in late November 1957, I would go back to New York and its famed garment district and learn about the ladies' wear industry. The date of my return to Switzerland was timed to coincide with Aunt Selma's 75th birthday in July 1959.

There was, for the moment, only one major problem: My mother was yet to be informed. I couldn't wait until my arrival back in New York because—in the interest of time—certain arrangements had to be made prior to my return. So I sat down and wrote my mother a letter. She was not a happy camper. It came as a complete shock to her. Her reply was a plea for me to abandon my plans and proceed with graduate school or law school or begin a job/career in New York. My mother always wanted me to become an accountant. I replied that we would discuss everything upon my discharge and arrival in New York. With continued ambiguous feelings toward my stepfather, I did not wish to remain at the Wetherole Street apartment, or live in New York. I happen to agree with the popular opinion that New York is a nice place to visit, but not a place to live and raise a family. Prior to my departure for military duty, I sensed and experienced my mother's unhappiness in her marriage. At this point in late 1957, I did not think that the marriage would last. I did not want my mother, following her hard times, to work for the rest of her life. I concluded that I could financially support her far better by working for the Neuburgers. Failing to change my mind, Mother wrote a desperate letter to Hanns, who in turn replied in a calm and reasoned fashion. Hanns' letter, dated November 4, 1957, also survived, and will appear in translation below.

"Dear Kate,

Today, I wish to address some personal remarks to you since you seem to be having considerable difficulties in processing Ernest's plans. I believe that you are seeing the entire scenario through an unnecessarily dark and pessimistic prism. In this day and age there are no more distances. Air travel has become routine and gets less expensive with every passing year. In today's technically advanced world, there is a continual need to stay on top of things and to develop all markets. It will afford Ernest the opportunity to travel to America on a regular basis. And, on the other hand, I hope that you will visit Switzerland regularly. It is my intent to offer Ernest every opportunity to develop a position in our firm that will give him the financial freedom to afford all that. Furthermore, and in view of the present global political scene*, Ernest and I agreed that he would not burn any bridges with his American connections, and that all channels and opportunities be kept in tact. Ernest and I have, and have always had, a wonderful personal relationship, and I am certain that our decision will serve both of us well. On the other hand, I totally understand your objections. I understand that you are concerned with the distance that will separate you from your dear Ernest, and that you would prefer to have him near you. In view of the fact that Ernest always told me that he did not intend to settle down in New York, I hope that—given a little time—you will get used to the general idea of our plans. Since Ernest's discharge from the Army is still several weeks off, it affords us the opportunity to continue our correspondence. I also understand your somewhat scary initial shock. However, I would suggest that, at least for the moment, you do not worry too much about this matter.

Yours, Hanns."

[*Note: You may remember my earlier reference that in the Fifties some Europeans still feared a Russian invasion of The West.]

Upon my return to New York, I took simultaneous courses at one of the "fashion schools" for about six months. I then obtained a position at Henry Rosenfeld, the hottest ladies' sportswear house on Seventh Avenue. I did live with mother and Edmond. However, I was on the Neuburger payroll from day one. I had told Hanns that I refused to continue to live in gentile poverty just to make the "grand plan" work. He agreed. The Army shipped over my Chevy, and I proceeded to have a pretty good time in New York for that year-and-a half, with my old college friends and my new Army buddies, particularly Bill, his family, and his new girl friend Dolores. My training and my temporary job went well. In June of 1957, as planned, I quit the job and took a vacation in Florida, prepared to leave for Switzerland in July. While in Florida, I received a telegram that Aunt Selma had suddenly—and totally unexpectedly—passed away. Much saddened, I returned to New York. I believe that Aunt Selma's demise made my parting from my mother somewhat more difficult. Aunt Selma would have been a steadying influence. I would have moved into what had in the intermittent years became "my old room", had the advantage of three square meals a day, plus the company of a caring, dear soul. It was not to be. I proceeded to Switzerland as planned.

Hanns picked me up at the airport as usual. On the one-hour drive to St. Gallen, he told me that the family mansion was undergoing massive renovation, but that I should live there until the work was completed, having all the advantages of Wally, the housekeeper, who was being retained as his, and his family's housekeeper. At that time, I would move into a new bachelor apartment that was in the process of being built for me on the formerly vacant top floor of the apartment house he owned. Just a few blocks away from the family mansion, his luxurious, full-floor apartment was in this house. He asked me if I had left any entangling romantic interests in New York, in other words, someone who might be following me. If so, I could always have his apartment. The new one-bedroom apartment could always be rented. I told him that no one was following me. Sadly discussing Aunt Selma's last days, we moved on and enthusiastically talked about the future, specifically about my impending entry into the Neuburger firm. With August 1st, the Swiss Independence Day, just ahead, the firm would be closed for two weeks for the annual summer vacation. I would, therefore, start immediately thereafter. So, why not take a little vacation trip ourselves? Why not, indeed. As usual, once again, Vera and Hanns and I headed for the French Riviera.

Finally, very early on a Monday morning in mid-August, real life at "Deneco" (D. Neuburger & Co.) finally began joyously. All the old, loyal personnel were still in place. I was simply greeting my old friends, many of them dating back to when I was eight or nine years old. They could not have been kinder or more welcoming. They had expected this for a long time. I would not be a threat to their positions, their duties, nor their supervisory authority. All would go smoothly—with the old, accustomed warm sense of humor—and it did! Hanns felt that his weakness in the business had always been in the manufacturing end. And, manufacturing was what I emphasized in my training in New York. I almost immediately made a business trip to Germany to look at some new equipment. (It was not for us.) Without great resistance, I introduced a few modern and advanced concepts that I had learned in New York. Although I expected to keep a close eye on manufacturing, I became too much immersed in this part of the business. Administration and merchandizing were more my *forte.*

Life in the mansion was spoiling me. The workmen were on their lunch break when I returned home at about 12:30. So it was nice and quiet and *sans* all that dust. In Europe, the two-hour-or-more lunch hour was still being practiced. Unless I had lunch with Hanns and his family, Wally would prepare a fine meal. Returning at about 6:30 in the evening, again the workmen long gone, a considerably smaller, informal meal would be ready for me. And, Hanns kept the wine cellar well stocked. However, being served and eating alone in the dining room with my two German-language newspapers and soon the European edition of the New York Herald Tribune did seem a bit strange. Almost immediately a certain loneliness started to set in. My classmate, Heinz, had moved to a small town at Lake Constance. Marion was expecting the return of her childhood sweetheart from South America, where he was being trained for his entrance into her father's business. George, Vera's brother, would only be in St. Gallen on weekends and the occasional weekday evening. He worked near Zurich. I needed the company of people my age. The work at the mansion and at the apartment ended simultaneously. Hanns saw to that. He should have been an architect. And perhaps he would have been had it not been for the untimely demise of Uncle David. It was time for me to move. Furniture from the mansion was transported to the apartment, as were rugs, bed, table linen, cookware, dishes and flatware . . . simply everything required to establish a new household. However, who would cook, clean, wash? "Aha, you need a maid," said Hanns and Vera. "What for?" I replied. "I can do all that." "In Europe, one has a maid," was the reply. And so the former maid of Vera's parents, now in semi-retirement, was summoned. She would come on Monday, Wednesday and Friday afternoons. She would make my bed, clean the kitchen and bathroom and wash my socks. At lunchtime on Wednesdays, I would take home a vacuum cleaner from the office and return it the next morning. All laundry, except my socks, would be "outsourced". Towards the end of my first week in the apartment, I came upon Vera finishing the last little details of my move. That was the drill: Everything would be taken care of. But, where was my independence, my privacy, the opportunity for my own tastes and imprimatur?

Meanwhile, at Deneco, we did not get out of the starting gate smoothly, effortlessly, nor speedily. There was a wide gap between Hanns' expectation and vision for my role in the firm . . . and mine. By mid-winter, I realized that I had most likely made a huge mistake by returning to Switzerland. This situation was further complicated by the continued constant *social* interaction between us. It's difficult to have disagreements at the office and then sit down for a good steak dinner and a fine bottle of Bordeaux. But we did it anyway.

Hanns had planned to build a new factory-and-office building at a new, yet very convenient, location. By early spring, the work began. This brought us closer together once again. We both had the blueprints pretty much in our heads bringing about much more collaborative work. The seas calmed, so to speak. Further, one of the administrative supervisors resigned, making my control of that area more secure. Actually, it went very well. My social life also improved immensely. Nevertheless, I remained depressed. I felt like a fish out of water. I was the only one in this town, population 60,000, who wore button-down shirts; the only one who knew who Yogi Berra was. I had difficulties mastering the Swiss dialect that I once knew so perfectly. It became more obvious to me with every passing day that "the great experiment" was floundering. I advised Hanns that I planned to take a paid four-week summer vacation in the U.S. (Round-trip airfare paid by the company, of course.) Two weeks were set aside to spend with my mother (and Edmond). The other two weeks would be set aside for job hunting and networking. I told him that I had not made a definite decision about leaving Switzerland, that I would be back in time for our plant re-opening in mid-August, and that I would not abandon the new plant building project until it was completed in late February of the following year, 1961. He was not surprised. He expressed the opinion that my plan was sound, but then quickly and surprisingly added that I was absolutely welcome to stay either for a protracted period of time or permanently as originally planned. This was, of course, an indication of our newly reconstructed "posture of good feelings", as well as a vote of confidence upon finally finding my sea legs at Deneco. However, this was no longer the crux of the matter. In truth, I was not able to re-assimilate into a smallish, provincial, somewhat Germanic town where everyone knew your business and everything was taken care of for you, down to someone washing and polishing my company car. Perhaps had it been in Zurich or Geneva, where there were still somewhat vibrant Jewish and American expatriate communities, all this may have worked. Sure, the salary and the perks were outstanding. As for my social life, everything was great. However, I would have surely married a Christian woman, since all of the Jewish youth had left St. Gallen, mainly for offshore locations, particularly Israel. Even my Swiss friend, George, was to leave just a few weeks before me that February 1961 to permanently live in Australia.

While in America I thought that the offer I received from Alfred's employer, a large, prestigious men's tailored clothing manufacturer, was the most interesting. I went to Baltimore for the interview and was hired by the firm's executive vice president with the understanding that I was returning to Switzerland and would not be able to start until March 1st of the following year. Upon my return to Switzerland, everything went as smooth as silk. I had a lot of fun at work and socially. The new office-factory building was completed as scheduled. I delayed my February departure for a few days in order to attend Marion's wedding. I then "cruised" to New York, departing from Genoa by ship, with stops in Barcelona and Casablanca. On the first weekend in March, I departed New York for Baltimore and started my job at J. Schoeneman, Inc. the following Monday morning.

I was happy to be back in America. It was then—and remains—the only country I could live in. I do not subscribe to the gloom and doom as it applies to today's America. I do not believe that America has its greatest days behind it. Although the governance of the country during the last decade may have been poor—both in Washington and on Wall Street—I strongly believe in the strengths of the American people: their freedom-loving spirit, their continued friendly openness and entrepreneurship, and finally their personal generosity and decency.

I still live in Baltimore, with my lovely, loyal wife of 42 years, our ever-esteemed children Jon and Leslie (and our son-in-law Jeffrey), and our two dearest granddaughters, Abbi and Julia. Oh, and a dog named Benji. Upon my return to America, I mended my fences with my stepfather, Edmond, and we eventually became extremely good friends. My mother seemed happier too. The marriage lasted for thirty-two years and included annual vacation trips to Europe and Israel, including regular Haas Clan reunions in Switzerland and—for special family occasions—in America. The former enabled my mother to maintain the contact with the Neuburgers, see their family grow, and stoke the warm friendship that remains to this very day. (I, too, made several business trips to Europe and always managed a weekend in St. Gallen.) In the summer of 1984, after Edmond had recovered from grave illness and long hospitalization, he and mother moved to Baltimore. Sadly, Edmond passed away six months later, leaving my mother widowed for the second time. As always, mother adjusted and persevered. Here in Baltimore, she had family, made new friends, had a lovely apartment, played bridge, went to concerts, enjoyed dining out, traveled far . . . and frequently, and generally enjoyed every day of her new life. Now, at age 101, she lives at a fine residence for seniors. She remains in excellent physical health. She is loved by all who cross her path. What else would you expect?

CHAPTER 17

A Final Return to Mannheim

"You Can Never Go Home Again."
Tom Wolfe
(He's right!)

As a final entry, I briefly wish to add that in 1991 my mother was invited
by the mayor, *der Herr Oberbuergermeister*, and the City of Mannheim to
visit her hometown for a two-week all-expenses-paid stay. She was permitted
to bring along a companion, which turned out to be me. My mother had
only been back to Mannheim once before to visit her father's grave. It was
a double grave that he would for all eternity occupy alone. It was during
this trip that my mother had my father's name engraved on the tombstone
to further record and remember his martyred life. She also wanted to make
certain that the grave—and in general the old Jewish cemetery going back to
the 15th Century—was well kept and would be in perpetuity. Accompanied
by Edmond and her first cousin Edgar from Strasbourg, she stayed only
a very short time, not even overnight. She did not feel comfortable on
German soil. However, so many years later, she reluctantly decided to accept
the generous offer from the Mannheim authorities and people. She was
eighty-three years old. The trip was a mixed bag. We arrived in Mannheim
to find very marginal accommodations at a hotel near the railway station.
The planners of this "friendship"/ "y'all come back" trip had booked only
one room, which they wanted Mother and me to share. I refused. They
said that the hotel was fully booked. Upon advising my German hosts that
I would move to another hotel at once, they suddenly did find a vacancy
at the hotel. The American attendees at this . . . let's call it a homecoming,

a group of about thirty persons, was also disappointing to my mother, for there were many who were really not "old *Mannheimers*". Rather, they represented families who had moved to Mannheim in the early thirties to escape early persecution in the provinces and to the East. The few genuine Mannheimers were of no great interest to my mother. She did not know them in her youth and too many years had elapsed to really find common ground. Yet, like most groups, this group did coalesce to some degree and produced some pleasant moments. Most of the evening meals and a few luncheons, usually attended by high ranking officials of the city, were excellent, as were the sight-seeing plans and the evening entertainment—including attending an opera performance at Mannheim's new, very (too) modern opera house. There was a day trip to beautiful—now almost suburban—Heidelberg. In addition to the German officials, both governmental and cultural, the members of the almost all-Gentile Mannheim branch of the German-Israel Friendship Society played a very large role at these functions. They were indeed very nice, genuine, sincere people. They visited Israel almost annually and were most forthcoming. My mother and I were immediately befriended by a middle-aged woman and her mother, with whom my mother and I corresponded until two years ago when she apparently died. (My mother's cemetery duties mentioned above were facilitated by one of a very few Jewish *Mannheimer* acquaintances who had returned to Mannheim after the war. He had no other place to turn to, he said. He was most helpful.)

However, in general, my mother and I felt very uncomfortable in public, especially while part of the group, which attracted stares from passersby and fellow street car passengers. It was very obvious to my mother (and me) that the average citizen of the city of Mannheim could easily have managed without our presence. Also, they probably resented the public expense of these annual shows of hospitality and contrition, faux or otherwise. I felt so uncomfortable that I took the weekend off and took a train to St. Gallen to visit Hanns and Vera Neuburger and their family. I don't think the Germans liked that. Neither did my mother. On the group picture taken in my absence, she looks tired and haggard. Upon my return, our German group guide, a young man who really tried hard to make this whole thing fly, asked for volunteers to join a panel to address a group of German high school students. They wanted us to tell of our personal Holocaust experiences, and opine on the Holocaust's affect on modern history. My mother volunteered, which meant I had to accompany her . . . and frankly, I did not object. When the six of us—and our guide—arrived at *Lieselotte* High School, the two senior history classes awaited us in a small lecture hall. We were warmly, but somewhat officiously, greeted by the principal, the head of the history department, and the teachers of the two classes. A panel table had been set up in the front of the room. The students, about seventy, more girls than boys, waited in a quiet, orderly manner. While each of us presented our stories of forced emigration, flight, suffering, loss and survival, you could hear a pin drop. These youngsters were obviously interested, surprised, attentive and courteous. When the question and answer period began they asked intelligent questions and accepted each reply with considerable grace. However, front row center, sat a young man of a different ilk. I had my eye on him for some time. He was blond, lean, and Aryan-handsome. His body language was aggressively forward, his blue/green eyes piercing. His questions were pointed and not all our answers acceptable. I was absolutely certain that if some neo-Nazi *Hitlerjugend* (Youth for Hitler) were to be reactivated the very next day, this little prick would be the first on line. He reinforced my negative perception of belonging in this place and time. Mercifully, the trip ended with an outstanding official farewell dinner that included the mayor and his entourage, official and unofficial, including his wife. Their façade was mannerly enough. However, behind it lurked the curse "Shit, next year we have to do this again!" Mother's and my final conclusion: Never again! Upon our return, mother and I, so many years after our initial arrival in New York, were once again prepared to kiss that good old American soil and behold the friendly, content faces of our fellow Americans. The airport sound system was pounding out an old Sinatra song, while the sun was shining brightly through the skylights and the Stars and Stripes fluttered outside. *This* was indisputably home. And weren't we fortunate?

EPILOGUE

Part I

In concluding this book, I hereby wish to state my personal views on the Holocaust.

First, I do not like the very name "Holocaust". It is not really the name, for "what's in a name," the Bard famously wrote. It is the one-word concept that I do not like. How can one word describe the enormity of the German nation's crime against humanity? It cannot! To better understand this entire issue let us begin with a definition.

Genocide. Hitler understood the term correctly, for literally it means "murder of a race". It applies to the intentional destruction, or attempted destruction, of a national, ethnic, racial, or religious group. Hitler incorrectly, and with intended malice, labeled the Jews as a race. Of course, we all know that Jews are not a separate race. Jews are Caucasians with a specific religious doctrine, history and tradition, and have inhabited Europe since the Days of Rome.

There have been examples of large-scale genocide throughout the annals of history, ancient and modern. In recent times, the Twentieth Century was sporadically interrupted by such "political" violence: The victims—among others—were the Armenians, the Ukrainians, the Kurds, the Bosnians, the Tutsis, the people of Darfur and the Sudan, and the victims of the Khemer Rouge campaign of extermination under Pol Pot.

And then, there were the Jews. Never before in recorded history had genocide been practiced on the minutely planned, efficiency-driven, result-oriented, industrial scale as the malevolent efforts of the German nation from 1933 to 1945, finally exploding into an impressive assembly-line-efficient orgy of mass murder from 1939 to 1945.

Consider some of these figures:

October 1940—30,000 Jews are deported from Baden (Mannheim is in the state of Baden.), the Saar, and the Alsace.

November 1940—(1) The Krakow Ghetto, containing 70,000 Jews, is sealed off.
(2) The Warsaw Ghetto, containing 400,000 Jews is sealed off.
In time, they would both be totally "liquidated"!

August to December 1941—70,000 Romanian Jews perish.

September 27/28, 1941—23,000 Jews killed at Kamenets-Podolsk, in the Ukraine.
At this time, in order to "protect" their own troops from such horrendous duty, and keep them combat ready, the German Army High Command approved the *Einsatztruppen,* special SS Murder Units, under the command of Reinhard Heidrich. They personally shot their victims and—more importantly—supervised the action of local police and troops in the occupied countries. These units soon grew to the equivalent of four companies. Just one of these companies, Group B, reported a tally of 45,000 Jews killed by November 1941.

June 1942—The SS report that 100,000 Jews have been "processed" in mobile gas vans.

June 30, 1942—The New York Times and the London Daily Telegraph report that over one million Jews have already been killed by the Nazis.

July 1942—75,000 Jews living in France, free or interned, including 11,000 children, and including my father, are deported to Auschwitz and two other death camps.

November 1942—170,000 Jews are killed in the vicinity of Bialystok. (. . . and you thought Bialystok was the name of a character in a popular musical . . . or a bagel.)

December 1942—Exterminations at Belzec cease after 600,000 Jews have been murdered. The camp is dismantled, plowed over and planted.

March/April 1943—Three newly built gas chambers and crematories open at Auschwitz. In total the four have a *daily* capacity of 4756 bodies! Soon thereafter, the camp is sub-divided into over thirty sub-camps.

April 1943—(1) Chelmo reports 300,000 deaths since inception.

(2) Treblinka reports 870,000 deaths since inception.

(3) Sobibor reports 250,000 deaths since inception.

November 3, 1943—Nazis carry out Operation Harvest Festival in occupied Poland, killing 42,000 Jews.

March 1944—Eichman, along with his Gestapo Special Section Commandos, famously arrives in Hungary to personally supervise the heretofore lagging extermination and deportation of Hungary's Jews. Upon their arrival in Auschwitz, 100,000 are gassed within one week. Within weeks, an additional 380,000 arrive from Hungary.

July/August 1944—Once the Allies have landed in Normandy, Hitler consciously increases all efforts of annihilation and murder of European Jewry. He suspects that he is going to lose one war, but still hopes to "win" the other. As proof thereof, Auschwitz-Birkenau records its highest-ever *daily* number of persons gassed and burned at just over 9000!

Enough statistics?

Soviet liberation of concentration camps in the eastern sector begins on July 1944. When Auschwitz is finally liberated, it is estimated that two million persons, 75% of which were Jews, had been murdered there. But, the Nazis never give up. After this date, 60,000 Jews are sent from the Lodz ghetto to Auschwitz. In November, 75,000 Jews are subjected to two death marches of over 100 miles in rain and snow from Hungary to Mathausen in Austria. Starving and hopelessly ill, few survive. There would be more such death marches as the Western Allies advanced. Finally, the mindless slaughter ends when the Nazi regime ends and Hitler commits suicide in his Berlin bunker on April 30, 1945. The two Bush presidents added the phrase "axis of evil" to our populist lexicon. There has never been a more evil societary entity than the German nation!

Part II

We hardly need to discuss the subject of Holocaust Denial and its mercurial machinations, except to express our desperation and rage. Unfortunately, Holocaust Denial is practiced not only by the vast majority of radical Islamists, but also—for example—in Orange County, California, as well. The mentors of ignorance, hate and evil never rest. Their irresponsible, reckless, and ruinous zeal once again brings on a cultural disconnect.

Although I am deeply saddened by this odd topography, I am far more concerned with the early signs of revisionism in Jewish circles, particularly among holocaust survivors of my generation. Their soapbox oration goes as follows: "The German people have suffered long enough under a heavy and stifling blanket of guilt. The grandchildren are not responsible for the actions of their grandparents. Contemporary Germans must *save their past* . . . and we Jews must help them." Excuse me? . . . Not on my watch! The wounds are far too deep. My generation of survivors—the witnesses—can never play the 'forgive and forget' game. And, our children and grandchildren are still too close to the butchery and the atrocities committed against their parents and grandparents whose only crime was that they were born Jewish. Can I ever say "Yes, Fritz, your people murdered my father, an innocent man. And, your people chased my mother and me around Europe to a point of desperation and physical and mental exhaustion. So, now let's sit down and talk, and have coffee and cake". And, can my grown daughter and son do likewise? "You murdered my grandfather, who I never knew, you drove my father to the very limit of a child's capacity to absorb terror. He has suffered from post-traumatic stress disorder for his entire life. Hey, so what? Let's sit down and talk, and have a glass of your fine German beers." Do my fellow Holocaust survivors really expect that from us? If they do, they are—at best—living in an alternative universe.

As for my indictment of the German nation and its people between 1933 and 1945, let me insert that among a nation of monsters, there were the statistically-expected exceptions, both in the lay population and—for example—in the ranks of Christian clerics. Children were saved and adults were shielded. Their good deeds must, indeed, be thankfully acknowledged. In our own journeys—as described in this book—we benefited from the humanity of two German Army officers. However, the actual number of these acts of compassion was infinitesimally small, especially when applied to the administration of the death camps. We cannot be fooled by randomness in evaluating the character of a nation. For the most part, the German population remained strangely oblivious to the changing mood of the country. There was no rage engendered by the new political status quo. Incessant Nazi propaganda produced the Counterfeit Self. The inequities that soon ensnared their Jewish neighbors were of relatively small concern to the German *Volk*. They lustfully bit into the Nazi bait. They were intoxicably caught in its promises of grandeur and world domination by the Aryan *Uebermensch*. And it was this very event that could not materialize while there was a single Jew alive in Germany, in Europe, in all the world.

Cavalier, premature forgiveness also minimizes the "statistics" of the Holocaust. We are still standing amongst the burning flesh and the blood of men, women and children of our—and the previous generation(s). Oh, the children! Again, using the one-word concept and the Six Million statistic excludes the acknowledgment of the full loss of that unfortunate generation, for the loss of six million Jews was not all that was lost. It does not include the physically and mentally maimed; nor the sterile; nor the surviving children who would suffer from post-traumatic stress symptoms for the rest of their lives; nor the children whose lives were so hellishly impacted that *their* children were negatively affected. If not for the Holocaust, the six-million-plus would have produced uncounted millions of Jews. And by now, those would have spawned three generations of Jews. But that was not to be. Hitler's Holocaust most certainly halted and reversed the growth of the Jewish population in Europe and eventually throughout the world, making the Jewish percentile of global population even more infinitesimal.

In the aftermath of the Holocaust, and after the creation of the State of Israel, another fallacious argument (in my humble opinion) took root. It claims that the Jewish state could never have come to be without the Holocaust. Since activist Zionism dates back to the latter part of the 19th Century, that is of course nonsense. But, that notwithstanding, I would say that the price of six-million-plus Jewish souls is far too high just to re-acquire a Jewish homeland. The suggestion of equivalency trivializes the unprecedented loss of lives. It also suggests some form of divine intervention in the formation of history. Unfortunately, this attitude can be seen in a portion of Holocaust survivors' literature. For example, the recently published (2008) *Small Miracles of the Holocaust* by Yitta Halberstram and Judith Leventhal, expects the reader to faithfully believe in miracles and divine intervention. For example: Two long-separated concentration camp inmates meet twenty years later—without intervening contact—when—by chance—they become neighbors in a suburb of San Diego . . . or wherever. Divinely driven miracle? No, we cannot permit the influence of extreme religious orthodoxy and Jewish fundamentalism to indiscriminately undermine the greatest human tragedy in the history of civilized man in this manner. We cannot decry Muslim fundamentalism, yet accept Jewish fundamentalism.

In conclusion and summation of the massive, collaborative, demonic ethos of the German people, let me say that the average German's capacity to do the right thing was totally compromised. The well-worn excuse "we didn't know" is indeed hollow and self-serving. The German Jews did not live in ghettos. They lived in regular neighborhoods, in houses and apartments. A Gentile family to the right and to the left, Jews may have lived there for a generation or two. Yet, one morning their Jewish neighbor and supposed friend, their comrade in World War One, their buddy from the bicycle or swim club was gone . . . disappeared from the face of the earth. Where did he/they go? What happened? Soon an upwardly mobile functionary in the Nazi Party moved into this nicely furnished and comfortable former Jewish-owned home. That's how Hitler, and his gang of deviates, showered rewards on loyalists. Yet, everyone continued to claim that they "did not know". Bull! Dachau—the concentration camp—was located in the peaceful, quiet, leafy suburbs of Munich, a major German metropolis. Jewish men and women were routinely beaten, tortured and executed there every day, while the bells of the famous *Frauenmuenster* church could be heard in the distance. But no one knew. They believed in their *Fuehrer* and his promise: "This is our moment." The cunning, outrageous, oversimplified Nazi propaganda and the unbridled show of super-nationalism wove a web of blood lust around the German people . . . and they chose not to escape it. And where were those neighbors to the right and to the left now? They were engaged in a contest of who could raise their arm the highest in the satanic Hitler salute. *Sieg Heil!,* you bastards. And, now you want our forgiveness? As for mine, you'll just have to wait.

Finally, who really believes we're near the end of the story? Anti-Semitism, and its deft scapegoat technique, is rampant around the globe. The "Never Again!" slogan of the Jews of the world sounds just a bit less forceful, with perhaps just a hint of hollowness, than it did, say, after the Six Day War or after Entebbe. Israel is once again in mortal danger. However, pessimism is not a Jewish trait. In the presence of calamity and death, Jews celebrate life and recite the Kaddish. Perhaps the non-Jewish author, John Hersey, understood this subject better than we do. In his classic, *The Wall,* the tale of the battle to defend the Warsaw ghetto against armed Nazi annihilation, the leader of the remaining handful of young Jewish surviving freedom fighters, who would most likely not see the dawn of the following day, asks "So, what are our plans for tomorrow?" That is what it means to love life, liberty and democracy, and intellectual liberalism. That is what it means to be a Jew!

THE END

Edwards Brothers Malloy
Thorofare, NJ USA
February 26, 2014